March 13, 2016

Dear Robyn,

Thank you very much for your continued strong support for our NEF programs with SUNY. Working together, we CAN "make a difference" (our mission) in the lives of millions!

All the best!

Appu

**Also by Dr. Appu Kuttan**

*Management By Systems* (cyberlearning.org/MBS)

*From Digital Divide To Digital Opportunity*

*World Tennis Instruction Annual* (cyberlearning.org/tennis)

# HAPPY EXECUTIVE

## — *A Systems Approach*

## Nurturing Mind, Body and Soul

www.appuji.org
www.happyexecutive.org
www.cyberlearning.org
www.nefuniversity.org

## Dr. Appu Kuttan

Founder of *Cyberlearning*

Library of Congress Cataloging-In-Publication Data
ISBN-10: **0988868008**
EAN 13: **9780988868007**
Library of Congress Control Number: **2013915039**

*Dedicated to the Indian Executives and People:*
*May You Find Happiness!*

# CONTENTS

**PART III: A SYSTEMS APPROACH FOR A HAPPY INDIA**

Foreword by Justice V. R. KRISHNA IYER

Former Supreme Court Justice of India. Author of over 70 books and hundreds of articles.

Revered in India as a national opinion leader, legend in jurisprudence and a "people's justice."

# Foreword

JUSTICE V. R. KRISHNA IYER

Dr. Appu Kuttan is an admirably able and inspirational advisor to all generations, especially the younger generation, a creative wonder, and a gift from Kerala, India, to the United States, India and the world.

Indian talent, when freed from the inhibitions of colonial-feudal Indian social structure, luminates in full splendour, catalysing the latent genius of our youth to bloom into excellence. In this sense, Dr. Appu Kuttan is an Indian gift and now a global asset. His fine book reveals how he began, as an outstanding academic and athletic engineering graduate from Kerala University, and then travelled to the United States to become a developmental wonder.

I first met him in the United States over 40 years ago as a brilliant adviser to the leaders of several countries. In 1980, he came to India as a volunteer to advise Rajiv Gandhi. He mentored Rajiv and taught Rajiv and many other Indian government leaders Management By Systems (MBS), his proprietary systems approach of using resources effectively to achieve goals, objectives, missions and visions, helping them become capable visionary administrators. At that time, as a Supreme Court Justice in Delhi, I had many discussions with him. At my suggestion to Delhi's Lieutenant Governor, he held luminous educative classes in Delhi for Indian leaders.

To hear Dr. Appu Kuttan speak, to talk with him and to read his writings is truly a process of enlightenment. His book is autobiographical and tells us how a bud does blossom. A few excerpts from his book will be apt and instructive. So I quote:

> *I was born the fourth of five children in Quilon* (now known as Kollam), *a town in the State of Kerala, India, in 1941. Both my parents were self-starters who pulled themselves up by their bootstraps. My mother, orphaned at a very young age, transformed herself into an educated, teacher-turned physician. She taught me the mental and physical gains found through yoga and meditation. I remember reading with her by the light of a kerosene lamp in elementary school as she emphasized the importance of academic excellence. My father, a renowned football player and athletic champion, was an officer in the state forest department. He introduced me to a daily morning exercise routine and encouraged my participation in football and athletics, with a focus on sprinting.*
>
> *When I was six years old, Mahatma Gandhi was assassinated, and on that day I vividly remember going with my grandmother to the temple to offer prayers. When I turned 14, I developed a keen interest in the Mahatma's writings and spent a whole summer vacation reading every book I could find to teach myself about his life, ideas and accomplishments. I was profoundly influenced by his thinking and his ability to develop and apply simple practical concepts by garnering the support of millions of Indians. His work taught me the importance of the four P's—Principles, Passion, Perseverance and Patience. His words, "a man is but the product of his thoughts; what he thinks, he becomes," and "the best way to find yourself is to lose yourself in the service of others," along with the influence of my parents as role models planted in me the seeds of the happy executive concept and lifestyle.*

The systems engineer in Dr. Appu Kuttan has been restless, always thinking positively and creatively. His systems-based holistic concepts inspire and enable the youth to emerge as a patriotic generation, original and inventive, no longer static but dynamic, capable of producing a transformation of our lethargic society into an activist one. Social engineering will be their new mission, beyond reading text books or traditional learning, but making radical change innovations and cultivate a passion to depart from tradition to technological advances. This is 'Kuttanism'. He is no longer just an Indian or American, but a global citizen who can help every country and person change for the better.

His book has many chapters, progressive and of fertile adventures. My purpose is brief and I do not go into the technical details, but I would like to emphasize on how he has converted dull, drab classroom lessons into modern developmental processes. He is an inspiration and incarnation. I recommend him and his books to every nation's leaders. He will advance their status. This is global patriotism. He is a glory for Humanity on our Earth.

# Preface

This book provides a simple practical pathway for everyone to live a healthy, happy and productive life every day. The concepts and practical steps described in this book are based on my experiences as a person and as a happy executive in India, America, Puerto Rico, Venezuela, Mauritius and other countries.

I spent my formative years in Mahatma Gandhi's post-Independence India, graduating in engineering as a top student, as well as the university athletics champion and football player. Later, I worked in higher education, and pursued my professional life as a management systems expert in America, India and other countries.

I developed the happy executive concepts in this book by applying **Management By Systems (MBS)**, an innovative systems approach I developed in the late 1960s while completing my doctorate in industrial engineering at the University of Wisconsin. **MBS is an integrated systems approach that leads to a Win-Win-Win situation, since it benefits all involved.**

The 21st century has brought a lot of changes, and I believe we need a new, progressive way of viewing the world around us, and operating within it.

My Management By Systems (MBS) Approach reflects this new perspective. MBS looks at everything as a system with specific goals and objectives. Then, it helps to develop the most cost-effective strategy and plan to make the best use of the available resources to meet those objectives and goals. The most important resource is the human resource, followed by financial, information, technology, physical, material and time. I explain this way of systems thinking more explicitly in Chapter 1 and Chapter 10.

Traditional thought usually views events or items as stand-alone entities. But by viewing them as elements of an inter-related system, those entities can be made more effective and efficient.

Many of these holistic ideas have been part of our Eastern philosophy. They are quickly becoming part of the new 21$^{st}$ century world view. For example, there is the spiritual belief that we are all part of one dynamic force or energy field. There is a new holistic scientific approach based on quantum physics. There is the view of global, rather than national economies. What happens in America or Europe or China or India affects people everywhere. We live in an inter-connected world today. We talk about the global economy and global warming.

The internet has played a large part in this globalization process, opening up new relationships between disparate groups working toward common goals. Just look at the important role social media played in the recent Arab spring events in the Middle East and the 2012 United States election.

The systems approach is especially timely, considering the recent colossal failure of the Wall Street financial firms to think through or be concerned about the chain effect of the highly complex mortgage derivatives. The piecemeal and reckless approach of these firms led the US and the world into American and global recession.

The autobiographical Part II of this book will introduce you to my systems approach and how I have applied it to governments, businesses and individuals. I have found MBS to be highly beneficial in all settings. **MBS** will help you not only in your professional career, but also in your personal life.

Over the last several decades, I have applied the MBS systems approach in several ways:

- I have advised many national leaders, helping to usher their countries into the 21st century. These achievements include using my systems approach in governments: bridging the East and the West successfully; and advising Mr. Rajiv Gandhi in the 1980s on creating a vision to make India an IT power.

- I applied this systems thinking to the individual by helping to develop three World tennis champions—Andre Agassi, Monica Seles and Jim Courier. My ideas of Total Tennis, the Happy Executive, and the Holistic Executive evolved from systems thinking about enhancing the individual.

- Later, when I moved on from the tennis academy, I took this concept a step further by donating my personal funds to found the non-profit National Education Foundation (NEF) in 1989. The NEF mission is to provide quality education to people everywhere, especially the underprivileged, using my systems approach. Having led NEF to become the national non-profit leader in the US in bridging the academic divides in schools, I have hopes that NEF will become a global non-profit, digital education leader in bridging the digital, academic and employment divides.

- Currently, I am also in the process of developing the Kuttan Preschool System. I believe that instilling the love of learning in young children, and helping them to develop a healthy mind–body–soul nurturing lifestyle from a very young age will lead to a better world.

- On a personal note, by using my systems approach, I have lived a full, healthy and happy life! I have been at work every day bright and early!

I am very proud of the fact that my wife and I raised a son and a daughter, who are very accomplished, caring and dedicated to serving and helping people.

I have practised yoga and meditation daily since the age of five. I have increased my workout by one minute every year—thus exercising 72 minutes every day now.

Throughout my lifetime, I have had the rare opportunity to work with all kinds of people, at all levels, in several countries in many diverse areas such as information technology, digital education, development, school and college education, healthcare, social security, transportation, traffic safety, and sports. The changes, especially in globalisation and technology that I have witnessed over the years, form the basis of my message in this book.

I am often referred to as the father of "cyberlearning," a term I coined in the early 1990s to describe learning via the Internet. I am told that my contribution to the English language is the word "cyberlearning."

As a result of my unique perspective and achievements, I have been asked by many to give some timely advice and guidance to Indian executives and youth, and hence, this book.

This book would not have been possible without the unconditional and active support, love and assistance of my wife Claudia, our son Roger (Raj), and our daughter Maya. I am also grateful to all others who assisted with this book, including Masood Huq, Tapan Chaki, Dr. Laurence Peters, Dr. William Diehl, Margaret Kale, and Tamara Stephens.

I dedicate this book to the Indian executives and non-executives alike, who can play a significant role in the welfare of India and the world in the 21st Century, to my family, to my dear departed parents, Narayanan Palpu and Dr. Narayani Lakshmi, and to Mahatma Gandhi. Both my parents and the Mahatma were my role models.

**Note**: This book provides excellent lifestyle guidelines. It is not intended as a substitute for medical advice. If you are taking medication of any kind, adding supplements or making dietary changes, a physician should be consulted before beginning any exercise program. The author specifically disclaims all responsibility for any liability, loss, or risk, personal or otherwise, which is incurred as a consequence, directly or indirectly, of the use and application of any of the contents of this book.

This book is current as of July, 2013, and as new information becomes available through research or experience, some of the information in this book may need modification. You should always seek the most up-to-date information and guidance on your exercise, medical care and treatment from your physician or healthcare professional.

# PART I:

## THE HAPPINESS SYSTEM

# CHAPTER 1

## A SIMPLE FORMULA FOR HAPPINESS

*"Remember, the past is gone, the future out there is unknown, and all we have is the present. Learn from the past, be mindful that the decisions you make now determine your happiness today and in the future."*

## DEFINITIONS OF HAPPINESS

The Dictionary defines happiness as a state of well-being and contentment coming from within.

*"Happiness is the meaning and purpose of life, the whole aim and end of human existence."*
– Aristotle

*"Happiness is when what you think, what you say, and what you do are in harmony."*
– Mahatma Gandhi

*"Genuine happiness mainly comes from our own attitude and spiritual qualities of love, compassion, patience, tolerance and forgiveness and so on. For it is these which provide both for our happiness and others' happiness."*
– Dalai Lama

*"A joyful heart is the inevitable result of a heart burning with love and kindness."*
– Mother Teresa

*"Nothing can bring you happiness but yourself."*
– Emerson

*"Most folks are about as happy as they make up their minds to be."*
– Abraham Lincoln

*"The happiness that is genuinely satisfying is accompanied by the fullest exercise of our faculties and the full realisation of the world in which we live."*
– Bertrand Russell

*"Happiness is a bundle of three main ideas: a pleasant life–having more positive than negative emotions; an engaged life–being completely absorbed by the challenges you face at work, love and play, etc.; a meaningful life–knowing what your highest strengths are and using them to belong to and serve something that is bigger than you are."*
– Martin Seligman.

## MY DEFINITION OF HAPPINESS

As you see, many people have defined happiness in many ways. I think of the human body as a most intricate and amazing system with billions of cells working in harmony to keep us healthy and happy!

Many people have asked me how I stay healthy, happy and productive every day. As I thought about this question, I realized that all my life I have applied the systems approach to happiness. I have tried to nurture all parts of my being—mind, body and soul—so I can stay happy and perform at my peak.

I am 72 years old, still healthy and happy. I have lived and worked in many countries with people of all ages and positions on a variety of programmes ranging from education and healthcare, to development, empowerment, cyberlearning and tennis.

I still work seven days a week, mostly as a philanthropist CEO, trying to make a difference in the lives of the less fortunate. I also work out 72 minutes a day—one minute for every year of my life on this Earth!

I enjoy thinking positively and creatively. I take pride in working out and eating healthy. I love to be caring, compassionate, loving, giving and nurturing.

These I call the Happy Executive concepts.

## THE SYSTEMS APPROACH TO HAPPINESS

How is it possible to apply the systems approach to happiness? First, let me explain my systems approach.

The innovative **Management By Systems (MBS)** approach I developed in the late 1960s looks at everything as a system. MBS requires you to set specific goals and objectives, and then make decisions about deploying available resources most cost-effectively to achieve those goals and objectives. The resources available are: human, financial, information, technology, physical, material, and time.

Everything, from a workstation to the universe, is a system. All of us— from the Presidents and Prime Ministers to simple workers—are systems people. Consciously or unconsciously, we set goals and objectives—daily, weekly, monthly, yearly or multi-yearly—and use all available resources to achieve them.

Of all the resources, the human resource is the most important, since humans in a system make all the major decisions. Financial resources are next in importance, followed by the other resources.

In designing or improving a system, first focus on getting the best human resources, then on finding the financial resources needed by looking at all options and by thinking out–of–the–box, and then on procuring and deploying the other resources.

Time is an important resource. Everyone has 24 hours a day. So, in order to stay ahead in the competitive global economy, plan and use your time effectively every day to achieve your goals and objectives.

There are **eight steps in applying MBS**: (1) defining clearly the visions, missions, goals and objectives; (2) mapping existing available resources; (3) assessing additional resources required to achieve the defined goals and objectives, (4) developing creative and out–of–the–box thinking solutions; (5) prioritising the solutions; (6) development of an implementation plan with specific tasks, milestones and timelines; (7) implementation; (8) monitoring and continuous improvement.

**MBS measures system performance using three measures, namely, effectiveness, efficiency and effort**. Always make sure that your system is effective, and then focus on making it more efficient, with sufficient effort.

Over the last few decades, I had the opportunity to apply MBS to improve socio-economic programmes as well as public and private sector and NGO operations—ranging from education, empowerment, traffic safety, social security, healthcare and information technology to tennis—in the United States, India, Venezuela, Puerto Rico, Mauritius, Egypt and other countries. See Part II, chapters 10 and 11 of this book for details.

It is worth noting that in India, I had the opportunity to explain to Mr. Rajiv Gandhi and other Indian leaders the MBS systems thinking, and help them apply it to develop India's vision to become an Information Technology (IT) power in the 1980s.

To learn more about MBS, visit www.cyberlearning.org/mbs.

## THE HAPPINESS SYSTEM — NURTURING MIND, BODY AND SOUL

Now, let us apply MBS to happiness. Looking at happiness as a system, your goal obviously is happiness. The resources you have are your mind, body and soul. Thus, from a systems standpoint, you can achieve your happiness or more happiness goal by nurturing your mind, body and soul.

## THE SIMPLE FORMULA FOR HAPPINESS

In my case, I have applied Management By Systems (MBS) to develop a happiness system. The simple formula I have practised for years as a person and as an executive seeking happiness can be summed up as follows:

First, find something you are passionate about doing. Second, when you go to sleep at night, ask yourself the following questions:

- Today, did I nurture my mind? Meaning, did I think positively and creatively throughout the day?

- Today, did I nurture my body? Meaning, did I consciously make decisions to eat healthy and do enjoyable physical activities to stay fit?

- Today, did I nurture my soul? Meaning, did I nurture other souls by acting in a loving, caring, helpful and compassionate manner with everyone I came across throughout the day?

- Today, did I perform activities leading to mind-body-soul balance—activities such as deep breathing, meditation, yoga, visualization, singing, smiling and laughing?

- Today, what did I do or experience that made me feel grateful?

If you answered yes to these five questions, you can feel confident that you were a happy person today, and you can look forward to an even better tomorrow!

Remember, the past is gone, the future out there is unknown, and all we have is the present. Learn from the past, and be mindful that the decisions you make now determine your happiness today and in the future.

Every morning when you wake up, remind yourself to practise the simple happiness activities covered by the above five questions. Take one day at a time in a simple, manageable manner. Your happy days will extend to happy weeks, months, years, decades and a lifetime! You will become a lifelong happy executive! And your happiness will radiate to others around you—your family, co-workers, friends and community members. In fact, this recipe for happiness applies to all human beings, executives and non-executives alike!

Of course, there will be bumps on the way. But the happy executive practices will help you reduce stress and smoothen the road to your happiness. We will discuss the pathways to living healthy and happy, by making appropriate changes in your lifestyle.

Based on my experience, my simple, straightforward advice is this: Nurture your mind daily by thinking positively and creatively. Nurture your body daily by eating healthy and engaging in physical activities that you enjoy. Nurture your soul daily by nurturing other souls around you—your family members, friends, employees, co-workers, community members and others you touch, by being caring, loving, sharing and compassionate.

I have practised these happy executive concepts for over 50 years. In the following chapters, I will provide you with the details of the simple and effective ways to find happiness by nurturing mind, body and soul, and maintaining mind-body-soul balance daily. I hope it will help you, as it has me, to reach your true happiness potential.

# CHAPTER 2

## NURTURING
## MIND

*"Think positively and creatively all the time, and enjoy doing so. As a creative thinker, you should not be afraid of problems; you should look at them as opportunities to come up with creative solutions. Often your creative solutions, based on "out–of–the–box" thinking, will produce better and more effective systems and solutions than tinkering with process-oriented piecemeal solutions."*

## POSITIVE THINKING

Remember the expression, "You are what you think you are!" The mind is the most complex and fascinating part of a person. It works like a super-fast TV screen, passing hundreds of thoughts, like images on film, every nanosecond. It works to instantaneously digest internal and external information, perceptions, senses, emotions and feelings, while continuously making and changing decisions.

The best and simplest way to nurture your mind is to think positively and creatively. According to Buddha, "All that we are is the result of what we have thought. If a man speaks or acts with a pure thought, happiness follows him like a shadow that never leaves."

When faced with stressful situations or with personal problems, positive thinking will generate positive energy and provide better outcomes. Negative thinking is like an avalanche, accelerating down a steep slope, building with immense speed and progressively worse consequences. By thinking positively, you influence your thoughts as well as the thoughts of those around you, thus creating a positive environment.

Although it may be challenging, it is important to make a conscious effort to nip a negative thought in the bud. If your thoughts have a tendency to be negative, it will be hard to see the positive. The mind is like an open field. If you walk toward the same destination, over time you will create a path. In the same way, you have spent much of your life thinking in certain ways about certain problems or situations and strengthening your mind's routine. Your mind makes thinking easy and does so by creating habits, getting from point A to point B along a familiar route. For this reason, it is difficult to change your mind state and try to think differently. However, if you practise redirecting your thoughts from negative to positive, you will create new neural pathways that will strengthen with more positive thinking. In time, your mind will make these tendencies unconsciously, and you will find yourself more of an optimist.

Think out loud and listen to your thoughts. How do they make you feel when you hear them? Are they positive? Are they negative? Address the problem by rephrasing your statement with a new tone or altering your approach. This will prevent the thought from developing into a negative one. Simultaneously, train your mind to see an alternative, positive side.

I remember it took a couple of years for me and others to counsel tennis star Monica Seles and her family back to positive thinking, after she was stabbed on courtside at the peak of her career. That incident taught me that even the direst of circumstances can be overcome with patience and positive thinking.

## CREATIVE THINKING

Sometimes we get stuck in old patterns and grooves, and we cannot seem to get out of our predicament, however positively we view the situation. It is time then to use more of our imagination, which is so active in children and young people and often atrophies in adults. Imagination is a great gift. According to Albert Einstein, "Imagination is everything. It is the preview of life's coming attractions. Logic will get you from A to B. Imagination will take you everywhere. The true sign of intelligence is not knowledge, but imagination."

Think positively and creatively all the time, and enjoy doing so. As a creative thinker, you will not be afraid of problems; you should look at them as opportunities to come up with creative solutions. Often your creative solutions, based on "out-of-the-box" thinking, will produce better and more effective systems and solutions than tinkering with process-oriented piecemeal solutions.

A case in point is our creative solution of distributing pensions through banks, rather than expanding government pension distribution centres in Venezuela. This saved millions of dollars for the government, while eliminating the waiting time to collect pensions for millions of Venezuelans!

Another example is my experience with developing world tennis champions. Instead of the conventional method of working on improving strokes, we decided to create a holistic total tennis system to improve mental toughness, physical conditioning, strategy and weapon strokes—the two or three dependable strokes one could call upon to win critical points. Then, we added tournament play and practice with the pros. This helped produce three world champions—Andre Agassi, Monica Seles and Jim Courier— in three years!

Studies show that positive and creative thinkers lead a better quality of life and live longer. You can be healthier, happier and more productive by practicing positive and creative thinking at all levels.

# CHAPTER 3

## NURTURING
## BODY

*"To become and stay healthy, eat healthy and do physical activities you enjoy regularly—at least three times a week; avoid unhealthy foods including excess salt, sugar, and saturated fat. Do not consume trans fat."*

## YOUR BODY AS A TEMPLE

Your body is your temple and can only meet its greatest potential when it is treated with respect. Only a healthy body can foster a healthy mind and soul. The human body is the most marvelous system, with billions of cells working together every microsecond to keep the body healthy! If the body can do this for you, shouldn't you take care of your body? Through proper diet and exercise, the energy taken into the body can be properly used, and the energy put out from the body will radiate in an attractive, positive way.

## EATING HEALTHY

When walking through any type of food market, you are inundated with a wide variety of products and options. When choosing among these products, it is important to read the contents of what is being purchased and how the item will help improve the function of your body. As a general rule, eat healthy calorie foods in the required amounts only, and limit the intake of saturated fat, sugar, salt, and other unhealthy calories, since such products will only stimulate the appetite, make your body feel bloated and sluggish, and negatively affect your mood. Avoid trans fat altogether.

Here are some points to remember when working to improve your diet:

- **Have a hearty breakfast, a moderate lunch and a light dinner.** Remember the expression, "Eat breakfast like a king, lunch like a prince and dinner like a pauper." By having your largest meal, rich in protein, at the beginning of the day, you are jump-starting your metabolism, providing the opportunity for your body to burn fat more quickly and your mind to work longer and more attentively. Furthermore, starting your day with a large meal can help reduce your calorie consumption, because your next meal will make you feel satisfied with less food. However, it is important to keep in mind the food choices you make during these mealtimes. Just because breakfast is the largest meal of the day, does not mean you should continue to eat after you feel full, or consume foods high in calories.

- **Avoid eating a late dinner.** Eating in the early evening hours is more effective for your body since, it enables a better quality sleep. When you wake up in the morning, you are starting with a large breakfast, because you are preparing yourself for the day. By early evening you should be winding down and preparing your body for sleep. Eating a large meal will keep your body from actively digesting, and will not give it time to rest. By having a small dinner early in the evening, you will find your quality of sleep is much better than if you eat a large dinner before going to bed.

- **If you feel hungry in between meals, have a healthy snack** rich in protein, complex carbohydrates and healthy fat such as a small handful of nuts. By eating healthy snacks between meals when you feel hungry, you maintain a steady speed at which your metabolism is burning calories. Your energy will remain consistent throughout the day, and you will avoid hunger which might lead to splurging or eating whatever is available, some of which could be poor quality foods.

- **Eat slowly and chew food well.** The digestive process begins in your mouth. By taking the time to chew food slowly and thoroughly, you prepare your body for a more efficient process of nutrient absorption. Consider consciously chewing each bite 20-30 times before you swallow.

- **Drink lots of boiled, cooled water when you wake up, and before, during and after exercise.** Drinking liquids regularly during the day prevents dehydration. Often, when you think you are hungry, when you think that you are craving food, you are really thirsty. Boiled, cooled water is the best drink. If you are already feeling thirsty, you are already dehydrated! If your urine is clear, you are drinking adequate liquids. If is dark, you need to drink more water.

- **Drink plenty of water.** Water has zero calories. Not only will drinking water make your body feel good, it may also satisfy mistaken food cravings. By drinking eight, 8-ounce glasses of water daily, you will improve your digestion, skin and temperament. Tea and coffee also count as a liquid; but beware of the caffeine in them, since they, along with alcohol, could be dehydrating. Be careful to minimize the sugar you put in your tea and coffee.

- **Drinking adequate liquids is also critical to thinning the blood and keeping it flowing.** This will lower the risk of a heart attack or a stroke and prevent damage to the major organs like the kidneys. It will reduce the likelihood of kidney stones. If you are prone to kidney stones, add fresh lemon to your water. Hydration is important for optimal functioning of your body and your brain.

- **If you are feeling overheated, dizzy or faint**, and it is because of dehydration, consume green coconut water, or fruit juice, with a banana to get electrolytes and potassium in your system. This oral re-hydration solution can help—add a pinch of salt with a couple pinches of sugar to a larger pitcher of clean water, boiled and then cooled, and drink it. This can save a life, maybe even your own.

- **Use less salt.** Too much salt makes you feel bloated and retains water. Salt also raises your blood pressure, putting you at risk for strokes and heart attack. In addition, salt ages you faster, both internally and externally, and shortens your life span. When you decrease the amount of salt in your diet, you will feel better and look slimmer.

- **Avoid adding sugar.** Additional sugar increases your desire for sugar, and will counter the satisfied feeling you want to maintain. Remember, you get enough sugar and salt from your normal food, so there is no need to add more.

- **Minimise the consumption of processed foods, unhealthy fast foods and junk foods.** Have you ever read the listing of ingredients of packaged foods? Regularly read the labels before you buy or eat packaged foods. Preservatives and additives are also in them, which are used to make foods last longer on the shelves of grocery stores. Remember, you want to take care of your body; the excessive amounts of salt, sugar, trans fat and saturated fat in these foods can cause serious harm.

- **Avoid soft drinks.** Soda or soft drinks, even the ones labeled diet, can create an imbalance in your body's pH level, in addition to extracting calcium from your bones. The consumption of sugar-sweetened soft drinks is associated with obesity, type two diabetes, dental cavities, and low nutrient levels.

- **Eat enough lean protein.** Protein works to build muscle and makes you feel fuller. You must be conscious of ways to add protein to your diet. Beans, lentils, legumes, eggs, nuts, seeds, fish (except fried), and dairy products are good protein sources. If you eat meat and poultry, make sure you are eating lean portions.

- **Eat plenty of vegetables and fruits.** Eat a variety of vegetables and fruits with all different colours daily. By eating fresh vegetables and fruits, you are consuming necessary vitamins, minerals, anti-oxidants and fibre. Vegetables and fruits, high in fibre, make you feel fuller. In fact, foods high in fibre help improve digestion and keep you feeling fuller longer because they take longer to digest.

- **Drinking a glass of low-fat or skim milk or eating yogurt daily is healthy.** Healthy dairy products are great sources of calcium and have also been shown to help you lose weight.

- **Eat healthy fats.** Nuts, seeds, avocados, seafood, olive oil, unrefined virgin coconut oil, fish oil and low-fat dairy and yogurt products are all good sources of healthy fats. Good fat is important in the diet for cell rejuvenation and energy, so do not exclude it, but consume in moderation. Limit the saturated fat in your diet. Avoid trans fat, anything hydrogenated or partially hydrogenated—it raises your "bad" (LDL) cholesterol and lowers your "good" (HDL) cholesterol.

- **Eat whole grains.** Whole grains have minerals. Essential parts of your balanced diet like fibre, magnesium and calcium are stripped when whole grains are processed into refined grains, making the product less healthy and nutritious.

- **Prepare food in a healthy way.** Preparing healthy food can be fun. Growing up in India, I watched my teacher-turned-physician mother routinely roasting spices in oil and adding them to most dishes for additional flavour. I have practised this cooking routine to this day! This is probably the easiest way to give any food an 'Indian' taste. Cooking is a good way to practise healthy food methods and will enable you to be more aware of what you are eating. You can make food more tasty and nutritious by adding healthy spices, herbs and other ingredients. Furthermore, spices have medicinal benefits. You can only gain from the practice of adding a variety of spices to your food.

- **Take a multivitamin tablet and a baby aspirin tablet daily, preferably after the evening meal.** Multivitamins are important to make up for any nutrients missing in your daily diet. Aspirin has been known to help prevent or reduce the incidence of heart attack, stroke and even cancer. However, some people should not take aspirin, so check with your physician first.

- **Make sure you are getting enough antioxidants and nutrients.** Vitamins A, C, E, Beta-carotene, Omega-3, and Vitamin D are disease-preventing nutrients that work to build the body's immune system. Consuming colorful vegetables and fruits is a sure way to provide your body with most of these nutrients. It is important to remember these changes are positive alterations, not dietary ultimatums. Making thoughtful choices leads to a conscious effort resulting in better body function and a clear mind.

- **Deal properly with emotional eating.** Remember, the food you are eating affects how your body and mind feel. If you find yourself eating when you are not hungry and making poor food choices, try reflecting on what you are thinking and how you are feeling. In becoming aware of your mind's voice and its relationship with your eating habits, you can address important emotional problems that may be causing you to seek out food for comfort. When you acknowledge your emotional eating, you can work to resolve the issues which influence your poor eating decisions. Do something physical, like taking a walk to reduce your stress. In time, you will find the weight melting off as the emotional stress lifts. You must love your body, since it is your own, and it is the only one you have! When you treat it with care and respect, you will radiate positive energy, charm and grace, and will be a more attractive and productive person.

- **Understand calories.** It is important to understand your calorie requirements in accordance with your exercise regime. If you are an athletic person, your body will need more energy to function better.

- **Keep a daily diary.** Write down what you are eating, how much, when, where, and why. Keeping a food diary has been shown to help people stay on track with their healthy eating goals. Also note the number of minutes of walking you do after every meal.

- **Avoid smoking altogether.** Smoking activates cancer cells and destroys your lungs. Being in a confined space where there are smokers also will put you at risk for cancer from second-hand smoke. Try other activities to occupy your mouth, like chewing gum, and do other activities to de-stress. There are always new medicines coming on the market to help people give up the habit. Do not give up trying. It often takes a couple of tries before a person can kick the habit.

- **Avoid excessive consumption of alcohol.** It is healthy for a man to have up to two, 5 ounce (141.75 grams), alcoholic drinks—such as red wine—per day, and a woman to have just one alcoholic drink per day. If the woman is petite drink less ounces. If the woman is pregnant then no alcohol. Anything more than that weakens the liver, and affects brain cells. If alcohol is addictive for you, try a program such as the alcoholics anonymous 12-step program, and stay away from places where there is drinking. Make new friends who do not drink for entertainment.

There is no happiness in destructive behaviors, but as soon as you stop smoking, and limit your alcohol consumption, your body will start to heal with good nutrition.

## PHYSICAL ACTIVITIES

Here are some things to consider when working to improve your physical strength and flexibility, stamina, vigor and vitality:

- **First, seek guidance from a qualified personal trainer or doctor.** These people are knowledgeable resources and they can help you. Ask questions and learn how to approach your exercise, and what specifically to do, especially if you have any medical conditions. You can also *Google* reputable sites for information before meeting the trainer or doctor.

- **Start slow.** If you are adding exercise to your daily routine, it is important to pace yourself. Jumping into an intense, drastic new programme may burn you out and lessen your desire to continue exercising. Additionally, you may find it hard to keep up and your attitude towards exercise may become resentful. Start with just a few minutes of activity you enjoy at a minimum of three times a week and set goals to add time and variety to your routine.

- **Alternate your activities.** The caloric output through physical activities including exercise is important for maintaining health and happiness. First, you can decide what kind of activities you enjoy—it could be walking, jogging, running, gardening, sports, swimming, dancing, weight training, or something else. You can alternate your activities and periodically change routines, then set a caloric output or time goal and work to meet it, all the while having fun along the way.

- **Choose activities and games you enjoy.** Working out should be fun. When you enjoy yourself while you exercise, you will continue to be physically more involved. You can also make your workout social by playing sports or inviting a friend along for a walk and run. Not only will time pass more quickly, but you will also be motivating your friend to take part in physical activities.

- **Increase your activity time as your body adjusts.** Your goal is to increase your activity level, meaning being more active, more often. When you are just beginning, you are working to build the muscles necessary to perform more strenuous tasks. By increasing your time gradually, you are working with your body to stay in shape and pushing yourself toward higher goals.

- **Try weight-training.** Weight-training is an important part of an exercise routine. Not only does it build the muscles you are strengthening, it increases your bone strength and elevates your metabolism, so that you can burn more calories from the same activities.

- **Keep a daily diary.** Write down your activities and how your mind and body feel before and after each exercise. This will help you to find out what you enjoy most and what makes your body feel best.

- **Warm up and then stretch.** It is important to remember to warm up before your work out and gently stretch only when your body is warm. Forgetting to stretch can stress your muscles and lead to injuries that will suspend your workout plan. Recent studies show that dynamic stretching—i.e., stretching while moving your body—is more effective than static stretching. It is interesting to note that my father used to tell me this years ago!

- **Get a massage.** Not only does massage relax you, it helps tone your muscles. If you cannot afford a professional massage, you can massage yourself by rubbing in small circles around your neck, legs, arms, etc. in the direction towards your heart. Deep breathing is like an internal massage, so remember to breathe deeply all the way into your stomach and then all the way out.

- **Exercise Routine.** My father was a famous Indian football star. He taught me my morning exercise routine when I was five. I am grateful for his guidance and the disciplined attitude towards exercise he instilled in me. Being a champion sprinter and football player throughout my years in school and college, I felt it important to continue with a workout routine after I graduated. This programme, the Kuttan Age Management Programme, makes me feel that I am in better shape than I was during the previous year, because I add a minute to my workout time every year. At age 40, I worked out 40 minutes a day. Now, at age 72, I work out 72 minutes a day!

- **Exercise.** I have helped design workout programmes for many top tennis players, including Andre Agassi and Monica Seles. I designed my own workout programme by integrating cardio and weight training. I call it "push-up-running." I turn on rhythmic music and assume a push-up or plank position on the ground. With my hands stationary, I run, bringing my foot forward under my abdomen, touching my toe to the ground below my belly button and extending it back, then switching legs. In intervals, I increase my speed to a sprint, and then decrease my speed to a jog. Every few minutes, I take a minute-long break. This exercise provides a rigorous cardio workout, strengthens my arms, legs and core body, as I balance my body weight between my hands and feet. For variety, I alternate this exercise with "jogging, running, jumping and sprinting on the spot" holding weights in both hands.

- **Aim for and maintain a healthy weight.** Weight control experts agree that there are common essential elements to effective weight loss and weight control plans. Healthy eating and proper exercise are essential to the balance between your daily caloric input and output. Set a goal of where you want to maintain your weight. Increase your energy caloric output by increasing your exercise, and decrease your caloric input by making more thoughtful food choices. You are working with your body to burn the energy stored, as fat, to lose weight. As you grow older, your metabolism rate decreases by 4% to 8% every decade due to muscle loss. This is part of the reason it is important to add weight training into your routine.

## FIVE LIFESAVING NUMBERS

Know the five lifesaving numbers for you and your loved ones: blood pressure, waist size, weight, blood cholesterol, and fasting blood sugar. Regularly check your numbers to take charge of your own health and stay out of danger. You will lessen the threat of life-threatening chronic diseases, and multiply your odds for health, happiness and longevity.

## BLOOD PRESSURE

Millions of adults have high blood pressure, also called hypertension. Maybe one-third to one-half of the people who have it, are not even aware that they have this serious medical condition. High blood pressure can cause many medical problems including cardiovascular disease, chronic kidney disease and stroke which can strike suddenly.

Get your blood pressure tested. Pay attention to the top number—the systolic pressure, which indicates the pressure when the heart beats while pumping blood—the best lifelong measurement for hypertension. If your systolic reading is above 140, it is considered too high, and you must see your doctor. You can buy a blood pressure measuring device you can use at home. Then, get in the habit of testing your blood pressure.

You can test yourself at different times of the day to determine when you feel most stressed. Then you can take immediate steps to do something about it, such as relaxation and meditation techniques, laughing, listening to soothing music and other activities.

Learn to use more spices and herbs and less salt. Salt raises your blood pressure, causing your heart to work faster and thus leading to heart disease.

Eating sugar, even if your weight is not an issue, directly impacts cholesterol and increases your blood pressure. This causes rigidity in the aorta, and puts extra strain on your heart.

Keep your resting heart rate below 90 beats per minute. You can determine your resting heart rate by counting the number of beats of your pulse per one minute. This number is a barometer of what's going on in the body. A slower resting heart rate means that your heart is more powerful and efficient.

Conversely, a higher heart rate indicates that your heart has to work harder to get the same things done. Studies have shown that women with a resting heart rate over 90 have triple the risk of dying from a heart attack, as compared to women with a resting heart rate under 60.

Luckily, there are things you can do to lower and stabilize your resting heart rate. One of the main reasons your heart rate speeds up is to fight inflammation. Instead of letting your heart do all the work, add healthy foods to your diet. Inflammation can also be emotional. In these situations, reduce your stress.

Your heart rate is also an indicator of your stamina level. You must exercise the muscle of the heart to keep it strong. During cardio workouts, you should aim to hit 80% of your max heart rate. You can calculate your max heart rate by subtracting your age from 220. For example, the target heart rate for a 30-year-old would be 190 x (.80) = 152. Reaching this heart rate for 20 minutes, three times a week will work to strengthen your heart. Remember to check with a health professional before starting a cardio program.

## WAIST SIZE

If your waist size, measured around your belly button, is greater than half your height, you are at risk of premature death, because belly fat creates and sends out a toxic, inflammatory stream of chemicals impacting the whole body.

Measure your waist all the way around at your belly button, not where your belt lies. In general, a waist size over 35 inches (90 centimetres) in women, and over 40 inches (102 centimetres) in men greatly increases the risk of chronic diseases like diabetes, heart disease and more.

## WEIGHT

Being overweight is often linked to belly fat, and is an indicator of coming or already existing health problems such as cardiovascular disease, gastro-esophageal reflux disease (GERD), gout, hypertension, high blood pressure and cancer. Weigh yourself first thing in the morning before you eat breakfast. Then, write it down. Studies show that by tracking your weight, you'll do a better job of keeping your weight in check.

## CHOLESTEROL

High cholesterol is a major risk factor for cardiovascular disease. You can find out your cholesterol levels with a simple blood test. Know your good cholesterol known as HDL, your bad cholesterol known as LDL, and your triglyceride numbers. Your HDL should be 50 or higher; your LDL should be under 100. Your triglyceride number should be under 150. A high triglyceride number means you are eating too much sugar or sweets, or foods like simple carbs made from white flour or even too much white rice. Simple carbs easily convert into sugar, causing your blood to become thickened like cream.

If your numbers are not in this ideal range, discuss strategies for improving them with a health care professional or dietitian. The more fibre you get in your diet, the more you are protected from heart attacks. Fibre acts like a magnet in your intestines; it pulls the cholesterol through your digestive system, before it can be absorbed in your bloodstream. Fibre allows you to deposit cholesterol in the toilet, instead of in your arteries. To get fibre into your diet, eat lots of vegetables and fruits. The liver produces cholesterol, therefore you want to eat foods that keep it healthy and avoid foods made from bleached white flour, added sugars, saturated fats and trans fats listed as hydrogenated or partially-hydrogenated fats. Trans fats are the worst, and can be found in many commercially packaged goods like cakes, cookies and crackers, along with many fried foods. Know the oils and fats used. Use mono-unsaturated healthy fats such as olive oil, unprocessed coconut oil, organic vegetable oils and nuts. Keep nuts handy for snacks.

## FASTING BLOOD SUGAR

Get your fasting blood sugar tested with a simple blood test or a finger stick test. This measures your risk for diabetes, a chronic disease that can lead to blindness, cardiac disease, kidney failure, nerve problems and an impaired immune system. You need to fast for at least eight hours to obtain an accurate fasting blood sugar number. Fasting is key, since eating any food, like a banana or drinking coffee or tea with sugar an hour beforehand, would raise blood sugar levels and could create a false pre-diabetic or false diabetic reading. If your fasting blood sugar number is above 100, you are now considered diabetic.

Lower your blood sugar levels by eating less sugary foods and less simple carbs like foods made from white flour. Eat more vegetables. Walk more. Add lemon juice or vinegar to what you're eating. The juice will make it easier for your body to process the sugars in your foods. You can also try adding half a teaspoon a day of cinnamon to your meals. It increases your body's sensitivity to insulin. Again, speak with a health care professional or dietitian to learn how to change your diet and exercise routine. Treatment measures should be discussed with a physician. Losing weight is the goal to bring down the numbers, if you are overweight.

I have maintained my weight in the 140-150 lbs (64-68 kg) range since I graduated from college in 1963. It is interesting and exciting for me to observe and balance my caloric intake and output daily. In the US, weight loss is a multimillion dollar industry.

Obesity has put serious strains on the United States' national health-care system. Promoting healthy eating and increased activity levels will improve the health and quality of life for everyone everywhere. Michelle Obama, America's First Lady, has recently launched a national program to do the same in the US.

Your health is very important. Healthy eating and physical activities are essential to become and stay healthy. They also stimulate the brain and help you to think and problem-solve better. To carry out these activities daily requires discipline and motivation. Building such traits contributes to success in business and related activities and, in addition, inspires family members, employees and others to lead a healthy life.

A happy executive can institute employee incentive programmes, promoting healthy eating and workout/exercise, much like the one we implemented at the Nick Bollettieri Tennis Academy in Florida. This, in turn, would make the employees healthier and happier and improve their performance. They can also be encouraged to extend the healthy eating and workout/exercise programmes to their families, friends and communities.

I am surprised that the recent heated health care reform debate in the US paid scant attention to preventive measures for obesity, such as healthy eating, physical activities and weight control. In recent conversations with several U.S. Senators, Congressmen and Obama Administration officials, I have repeatedly emphasised the need to promote preventative healthcare. For example, the growing diabetes epidemic in America, India and other countries is directly affected by the type and quantity of food being consumed and the lack of sufficient physical activity. Preventative measures such as promoting healthy eating, physical activities and physical education can help reduce health care costs significantly in the United States, India and other countries.

Without such preventive measures, the United States, India and other countries will face significant increases in healthcare costs affecting seriously their economies and quality of life.

# CHAPTER 4

## NURTURING
## SOUL

*"Nurture your soul by nurturing other souls—your family, friends and others. By practising love, compassion and selfless giving, you will also enhance the presence of your soul in your everyday experiences. All religions address the moral obligation of helping those in need."*

## MY BELIEFS ABOUT HAPPINESS

The Dalai Lama said, "The purpose of our lives is to be happy. If you want to be happy, or others to be happy, practise compassion. It is very important to generate a good attitude, a good heart, as much as possible." I believe that the best way to nurture your soul is to nurture the souls of others. *Namaste*, the traditional greeting in India with folded palms, recognises an eternal oneness and means the soul in me recognises and salutes the soul in you. By approaching everyone you interact with in a kind, caring, loving and compassionate manner, you will find happiness in addition to an abundance of friends.

As a serious student of Mahatma Gandhi in my formative days, I always believed that those who are fortunate enough to acquire money and power have a moral and ethical responsibility to share their wealth with the disadvantaged. When I sold the world-famous Nick Bollettieri Tennis Academy to the multi-billion dollar IMG sports management group, I gave the proceeds to the non-profit National Education Foundation (NEF) I founded to provide educational opportunities to those who could not afford them. As Mahatma Gandhi said, "Earth provides enough to satisfy every man's need, but not every man's greed." Such sharing gives me an opportunity to nurture millions of souls and I am thankful, indeed, for such an opportunity.

I believe that divinity is manifest in all living beings and all souls are connected in some way. The best way for you to nurture your soul is by nurturing other souls—those of your family members, friends, employees and anyone else you touch in your daily life. In order to nurture your soul, you have to recognise there is no difference between your soul and the souls of others. You must be disciplined in the practice of awareness, compassion, love and selflessness, and be open to being a leader by working with and for others.

When I was advising the Government of Venezuela, the maître d' of the Caracas Hilton hotel told me one day that, in all his years working at the Hilton, I was the only person he had seen bring top national leaders for dinner one evening and regular computer operators and office staff on another evening. I told him that I see the same human soul in everyone, irrespective of their positions, power, or money.

All religions have a concept of soul, but many tend to focus on the outward signs of spirituality without paying attention to nurturing the inner self. Prayer and observation of devotional practices are simple ways to acknowledge the divine element of the self. Additionally, by practising love, kindness, compassion and selflessness, you will also enhance the presence of your spirit in your everyday experience. All religions address the moral obligation of helping those in need. Sometimes it may be challenging to practice spirituality; however, with practice it will mesh into your personality.

My suggestions below will help you practice nurturing your soul.

## COMPASSION

A compassionate person is one who is able to empathise and sympathise with the feelings, experiences and hardships of others. A compassionate person is eager to be available to others and finds satisfaction in making a difference. It may be easy to be a compassionate person occasionally, though it may be challenging to get into the habit regularly. With practice, the behaviour will become second nature and you will be less aware of the fact that you are offering your assistance to others. Additionally, you will be fortifying the quality of your character, while nourishing your soul with the practices of kindness and goodness. By being kind and selfless, you will deepen your understanding of essential life lessons.

If you help one person every day, eventually you will be eager to help many, and kindness and selflessness will become part of your nature. Avoid thinking of self when it comes to helping others. Concentrating on what you are gaining is a negative way of thinking and will only contradict your practice. Doing something for someone else will be gratifying and uplifting. If you begin to consider such situations negatively and selfishly, it will be very difficult to grow into the open, kind and compassionate person you can be.

Through positive thinking and selfless actions, you help to build a tighter bond with people and deepen friendships. A person who is compassionate has an abundance of friends, people who can be relied upon in times of need. By working to help others, we are creating a more connected world built on mutual assistance. If you make someone else happy, you will also make yourself happy.

When you enter a state of happiness, you are at peace with the world. At the end of every day, it is wonderful to lie in bed, content with all that you were able to do and the goodness you created, by making yourself available to the needs of others. As you continue to live this way, you will find you are able to rest more peacefully at night and wake up more eager for the day's tasks. If you start your day by practising compassion and continue to challenge yourself to do good deeds for others, you will receive positive reinforcement for each task that has been completed, and you will want to continue to do this every day.

Your actions can be the source of another's happiness, and make that person feel grateful for being alive. Doing this every day will provide you with the foundation to lead a happy, balanced spiritual life. The soul is the part of the self that is eternal. It is the part of the experience of life that is connected to all other living beings and is the one thing that every living creature has in common. It is the essence and definition of being. If the soul is nurtured and treated well, the being will be compassionate; the being will be kind, caring, and aware of the entire world around it. When the soul is present with its fullest and greatest potential, the person will radiate a light and essence, an aura of goodness and energy to which all others will be attracted. People in touch with their inner souls have a sparkle in their eyes.

## LOVE

Remember the expression that love makes the world go around. Love is one of the most popular words used by humans. To be happy, you must love yourself first and all those whom you touch. When you love yourself, you actually love your entire self, as well as your strengths and weaknesses. Accept all you do and have done and embrace the fullness of who you are. When you love yourself, you are able to share the elation with all those around you. Think of the world as more than just what we see and feel, and of the moment as greater than how we are experiencing it. However, when we understand that our own minds function independently, we begin to recognise that life is all about perspective and we can advance our souls and ourselves by learning to concentrate on the positive. When we are optimistic and think life is gracious and beautiful, it will be. Because we can only think and feel how we allow ourselves to think and feel, we are in control of our state of consciousness.

If you love, you create love, causing a contagious effect where all persons continue to share an elevated, positive feeling. Love unconditionally. Don't be afraid of love. People spend so much of their time in fear, afraid of being hurt, heartbroken, separated or deceived. These people live negative lives and are only aware of the pains and heartaches they encounter and experience. A person who lives a life full of love is optimistic, earnest and positive. What is needed is the extension of our love to others—family members, friends, co-workers, community members, strangers and other members of our human family. We are all part of the same great existence, and if we live consciously in love, the scale will be tipped in positive favour for a more loving, unified world.

## FORGIVENESS

Guilt is the heaviest weight on our conscious mind and can come not only from within, but also from external experiences. To be freed from guilt, one must learn forgiveness and relieve the mind and heart of any and every self-imposed burden. We all make mistakes, and the greatest way to grow is to learn from our past. Born with an ego, we all have selfish desires. When we learn to understand our ego and listen to the voices of the heart and soul, we can become more familiar with the ego's voice and quiet its demand for attention.

To be truly content with yourself, you must be able to forgive. It's important to have experiences and to learn from consequences; however, if you do not learn to forgive, you will find yourself subjected to a weight on your heart that will prevent you from being able to open up and freely communicate and love. To begin practising forgiveness, start by having a genuine intention. Sincerity is an easy way to avoid imposing any weight on your conscience. When you are kind to someone, be true with your kindness. Remember to think of others before the self, and be willing to make sacrifices.

Practise forgiveness by forgiving yourself. If you feel ashamed, meditate on the feeling. Embrace the emotion and concentrate on how it feels. Eventually, you will clear your mind and understand what is making you feel ashamed. Once you have created an understanding, you can begin healing yourself through your forgiveness. It is easy to apologise, but to truly forgive you must let go of fear, anger and frustration and address the source of these emotions.

Do not focus on the past, focus on the present and prepare for the future. If you are troubled by something you have done, concentrate on why you made that decision. You will learn more about yourself, and through such understanding you will be able to forgive your actions. If you are unable to forgive, you will continue to live your life burdened by the past. So, forget the past, forgive and move on with your life. Once you know better, you will do better.

## GRATITUDE

Gratitude can be the shortest path to happiness. The more grateful you are, the happier you will feel. The miracle of gratitude is that it shifts your perception to such an extent that it changes the world you see. Gratitude changes your brain; it boosts your mental health. It is impossible to be simultaneously grateful and depressed. The more you practice gratitude, the more grateful you will be. The happiest people are the ones who appreciate life the most.

Start by writing down three simple things that you are grateful for and which make you happy. When you wake-up, it could be the rising sun, the chirping birds, looking into the eyes of someone you love, the opportunity to live another day. Make this a habit to do when you wake up and again before you go to bed. Consider the things you have done for others, things others have done for you and all those small acts of kindness that make you smile. Doing this before you go to bed even helps you to sleep better. After the first week, your mood will be boosted. Make this a regular habit, like brushing your teeth, and increase your list to five simple things.

Expressed gratitude is double happiness, because it makes both the giver and the receiver happier. Gratitude lessens anxiety and depression, neutralizes anger and bitterness, and increases your happiness. People who practice gratitude get healthier, happier, and expand their potential. They treat their loved ones, neighbors and people they meet on the street with more respect and consideration. Throughout history, philosophers and religious leaders espoused gratitude as a virtue integral to health and well-being.

## HELPING

If it looks like someone's task would be made easier by your helping, offer to help. Sometimes they will thank you and decline, while other times they will accept. If they accept, consider applying both of your creative minds, being thoughtful of how you can work together to solve the problem in the most effective way.

## LISTENING

Nurture the soul by listening. It is amazing how much more aware you will be of your present when you listen to what is going on around you. When you are aware, you enable yourself to pick up on life's subtle clues. Then, you will be able to take advantage of all the opportunities that are available to you. Create an environment for yourself, where you feel comfortable and happy. Surround yourself with kind people.

In summary, nurturing the soul can be a wonderful, rewarding experience for you and those around you. Every moment can be lived as it is experienced. To have a successful experience, understand that your purpose as a human being is to live a full life by helping others, being your best self and trying a little more and a little harder to make the world better. When you develop a heightened awareness, you will be amazed by how differently you experience the world around you. You will have a feeling of serenity, a tranquil calm—much like the feeling of lying on a warm, quiet beach when the sky is clear and the rays of the sun are keeping you in a steady, warm and gentle embrace.

# CHAPTER 5

## MAINTAINING MIND-BODY-SOUL BALANCE

*"Yoga, deep breathing, meditation, visualisation, sleeping, dancing, singing, smiling, laughing and any other enjoyable activities that you think of, can be practised individually or in groups to achieve the mind-body-soul balance. These activities will lead to your personal and professional happiness."*

## BALANCING MIND, BODY AND SOUL

Your soul is what you are, your body is what you have and your mind is the middle ground between your soul and body, the battleground for your conscious and subconscious decisions. It is the scale for your physical, emotional, spiritual, and mental self.

To find balance, you must understand and care for your mind, body and soul. Doing so will give the care and attention to all elements of your being or self system, and will allow you to find inner peace. Now that you know how to nurture the mind, body and soul, you can do activities to help find a harmonious balance. Such activities include yoga, deep controlled breathing, meditation, sleeping, visualisation, dancing, singing, smiling, laughing and other enjoyable activities.

## YOGA

The practice of yoga reconnects one with the universe more than any other type of exercise. It gives me a sense of renewal and awareness and centres me as I organise the start of every day. Doing simple stretches and practising poses allow me to work calmly with a clear mind and focus on the tasks I have to perform. You don't need to be a believer in any one religion or philosophy to understand that we are all, at a very elementary level, energy waves or particles, and as such, we are really part of the universe's spirit. With this understanding, it seems clear that we all share the obligation to create the best energy within ourselves to fuel and strengthen the greater energy of the universe.

Practising yoga stretching exercises on a regular basis helps keep the body nimble and the mind alert. Doing yoga stretches either in the morning, evening, or during work breaks will relax you, keeping you calm and alert. I have practised *Shirshasana* or "standing on the head" every morning for five to 10 minutes since the age of five without fail, indoors and outdoors, even on beaches, ships and airplanes.

*Shirshasana* is called the "king of *asanas,*" because of its overall effect on the body as a whole. In addition to increasing the blood flow to the brain, it helps one to deal with difficult situations with more equanimity. It makes me feel refreshed and energised. However, if you are a beginner, it is best to start against a wall or in a corner or lying in a slanted position. This way you can divert your attention from falling to balancing. Eventually you will find stability and be able to do it without support.

## DEEP, CONTROLLED BREATHING

Breath is what connects body, mind, and soul. According to an ancient Sanskrit saying, "For breath is life, and if you breathe well, you will live long on earth." We all breathe the same air. Many cultures and religions view breath as life—a divine connection binding us to one another and nature. Deep controlled breathing is often termed as the true essential exercise; it can be done anywhere at any time, at no cost with enormous benefits. Deep breathing is the simplest way to work toward the improvement of your mind-body connection and attain consistent happiness. Because you are constantly breathing, all you have to do is start consciously taking deep breaths, inhaling preferably through the nose and exhaling through your nose or mouth until it becomes second nature. If you take a few deep breaths periodically during the day, you will pump more oxygen into your lungs and rejuvenate your body and brain. Most people breathe with a third to a half of their lung capacity.

Deep breathing empties the carbon dioxide in all parts of the lungs and replaces it with fresh oxygen. This results in a relaxation response, a deeper relaxation with reduced level of stress and clearer thoughts. Deep breathing contributes to more energy, less fatigue, less stress, less anxiety and, believe it or not, even weight loss. Like what the heart is to your circulatory system, deep breathing is the pump for your lymphatic system. They work together as the blood flows, carrying nutrients and oxygen into your cells. A healthy lymphatic system carries out the destructive toxins, significantly improving the balanced functioning of your entire body.

There are many breathing techniques ranging from the simple deep breathing to the three-part or yogic deep breathing. You can simply fill your lungs fully through the nose, holding the breath for a few seconds, then, slowly exhaling through the nose at twice the time. For example, inhale in four seconds, hold the breath for four seconds, and exhale in eight seconds. Place a hand just above your belly button. If you're breathing deeply, your hand will rise and fall with each breath. Keep practising often, and you'll soon be breathing properly all the time.

When you inhale, expand your belly first, then your mid-torso and finally, your chest. When you exhale, contract the opposite way. You will feel the cycle of your breath moving through you as the end of your exhale becomes the beginning of an inhale and vice versa. The cycle is constant and, when you give it your full attention, it brings peaceful energy. Practising deep breathing while sitting comfortably straight, standing comfortably straight or walking leads to better health and happiness.

If you ever feel especially anxious or panic-stricken, breathe in through your nose to the mental count of three or four—whatever count you are comfortable with, and breathe out through the mouth to the mental count of six to 10—however long you can go, and that will help you to feel calmer.

I have practised deep breathing daily from the age of five, and I can attest to the benefits of deep breathing outlined above.

## MEDITATION

Meditation can be defined as "sleepless sleep." When you meditate, your goal is to keep your mind free of thought—just like in a state of sleep while being conscious. There are many ways to meditate. The simplest way is to sit in a quiet place with your eyes closed and spine comfortably straight, listening to your breathing, keeping the mind clear of thoughts. After a while, your breathing will sound like rhythmic music. If you find your mind wandering or distracted, redirect your focus to your breath. Some find it useful to repeat a sound or mantra like Om, or visualise something like a candle light in your mind's eye. Do whatever helps you to keep your mind calm and still. With practice, your meditation will improve and your will find your body and mind more relaxed.

Doing just five minutes of meditation in the morning can help alleviate stress all day. You can meditate before you start work, after you finish work, during a lunch break or whenever you feel you need a moment to be still and at peace. It is best to meditate uninterrupted and in a quiet place where you will not be distracted by the outside world. You will learn to really enjoy meditation as your experience its benefits. You can increase the length and number of times you practise as you wish.

Meditation helps you to relax, slows down your heart rate, lowers your blood pressure, lowers stress, stimulates your immune system, rejuvenates your mind and provides the opportunity to think more positively, creatively, and clearly.

Reducing stress in your life can dramatically impact your health and how long you live. In addition, research shows that meditation helps to grow brain cells at any age. I meditate 10 minutes each day in the morning, noon, and evening. I also meditate with deep breathing whenever I feel a build-up of stress.

## VISUALISATION

Visualisation is the practise of effecting performance outcomes by making mental pictures of desired outcomes. It is the basic technique underlying positive thinking and has been shown, particularly with athletes, to result in better performances. It can certainly be applied to goals in life and work and, as an executive; you can practise the visualisation of your professional path. I visualise outcomes when I take on a project or a task. I also visualise my tennis strokes every morning for a few minutes which helps me continue to improve when I am unable to play on a regular basis. Research shows visualisation and shadow strokes strengthen neural paths, muscle memory and brain focus. While I owned the Nick Bollettieri Tennis Academy in the 1980s, I had our players practise visualisation for match and point outcomes before every match and point.

It should be noted that one could combine deep breathing, meditation and visualisation. For example, you could meditate by listening to your breathing, while visualizing to be floating in the calm blue waters on a beautiful serene beach! You could add yoga to the equation if you assume a yogic pose, while doing deep breathing, meditation and visualisation.

## SLEEPING AND NAPPING

Getting adequate sleep is critical for health and optimum functioning, to feel more refreshed and energized, to think clearer and better, and to be happier. Anything less than seven or eight hours sleep is inadequate. Between seven to eight hours is ideal.

Do you feel refreshed when you wake up? If you do, then you are getting enough sleep. If not, increase your sleep time. What is the time you need to wake up? Is there anything you can do the evening before to make your morning routine go faster, so you can get more sleep time? Consider setting an alarm clock seven or eight hours before your wake up time, so you know when to go to bed to get adequate sleep. The darker you make the room, the better you will sleep. Cover the colored lights from alarm clocks, TV sets, etc.

If you snore at night, the snoring needs to be medically checked out for sleep apnea.

If you feel tired during the day, especially during the afternoon, perhaps you ate too much for lunch. Consider modifying your lunch to include more vegetables and fruits and less simple carbs and sugars.

Maybe you need a nap. Twenty minutes is the ideal time for a nap. Too long a nap may not be invigorating. Go somewhere where it is quiet and dark for your nap.

When you wake up, do some simple stretching exercises to get the blood flowing and pumping reinvigorating oxygen throughout your body and your brain. Einstein was famous for taking naps.

## DANCING

Dancing is the rhythmic movement of the body to music. Dancing to music rejuvenates body and mind, brings more oxygen to all parts of the body and lowers stress. Dancing is relaxing and therapeutic, and can be enjoyed in groups or independently. I dance to rhythmic American, Indian and Latin music for a few minutes quite often. I got interested in Latin music and dancing from my days in Puerto Rico and Venezuela.

Dancing is great because you can do it anytime or anywhere as long as you do not interfere with others. If you feel like dancing and are in a crowded place, you can practise it in your mind with visualisation, and feel the joy.

## SINGING, HUMMING AND PLAYING A MUSICAL INSTRUMENT OR JUST LISTENING TO MUSIC

Singing is defined as making musical sound with voice, especially word. Singing, humming, playing a musical instrument or listening to music, all of these have a number of health benefits. Research shows that these activities strengthen the immune system, makes people feel more energized and uplifted, stimulates circulation, and can help people breathe more deeply. Sing or hum or play a musical instrument or listen to music that makes you feel happy, whenever and wherever you can.

## SMILING AND LAUGHING

Smiling makes you happy instantly. Even at moments when you are not happy, smiling will help you to become more positive. A smile does not cost anything and yet, with a smile, you can put your entire environment at ease. It is a compassionate and elevating practise. Laughter is the audible expression of joy or happiness. As with smiling, laughter works to lighten the mood and is said to be the best healing medicine. You can laugh and smile and thus find many health benefits like lowered blood pressure, stronger cardiovascular function, reduced stress hormones, improved circulation, increased muscle flexion, better immune function and the release of endorphins—the body's natural painkillers. Thus laughing and smiling produce a general sense of well-being.

All these techniques—yoga, deep breathing, meditation, visualisation, sleeping, dancing, singing, smiling, laughing and any other enjoyable activities that you can think of, can be practised individually or in groups to achieve the mind–body–soul balance. They will help you reduce stress, and lead to increased personal and professional happiness.

I have practised these concepts and activities for years, helping me to lead a happy and productive life. I have always looked forward to every day. I attribute this attitude to my staying healthy, happy, positive, creative, nurturing and productive.

It need not be any different for you. As the famous Nike commercial rightly says, **"Just do it."**

# CHAPTER 6

# SEVEN "P's" TO SUCCESS AND HAPPINESS

*"Whatever you do, first establish your Purpose, then determine the best Pathway for you to get there, then carry out your program with Passion, Perseverance, Positivity, Patience and Principle—and you shall succeed!"*

## A CONCEPT TO LEAD YOU TO SUCCESS

Life is very complex. Yet, if Albert Einstein was able to define universal energy with a simple equation, $E = mc^2$, we should be able to come up with a simple concept leading to success and happiness in life's endeavours. That is why I have formulated the Seven "P's" for success and happiness, based on my own personal and professional experience.

The Seven "P's" are: **Purpose, Pathway, Passion, Perseverance, Positivity, Patience and Principles.**

## PURPOSE

Purpose is the most important of the Seven "P's". If you do not know your destination, how will you get there? Purpose is defined as the objective, result, end, goal or aim of an action intentionally undertaken. It must be meaningful to you and those beyond yourself. According to Helen Keller, happiness comes from "fidelity to a worthy purpose."

Both eastern and western philosophies emphasise the key role purpose plays in life. The *Bhagavad Gita* urges purposeful action or *karma* according to law or *dharma*. The Dalai Lama states that the "purpose of life is the pursuit of happiness." The "pursuit of happiness" is also an integral part of the famous United States' Declaration of Independence document.

In a recent book, *Purpose: The Starting Point of Great Companies*, by Nikos Mourkogiannis, he concludes that focusing on purpose leads to the four attributes of greatness—morale, innovation, competitive advantage and leadership.

Purpose includes visions, objectives and goals. A vision is the overall end result you wish to achieve for yourself, your family, your organisation or your community. Objective is the function that your efforts or actions are intended to attain. Goal is the specific numerical target you want to accomplish with a clear timeline.

For example, in designing the Prime Minister's Universal Information Communications Technology (ICT) program in 2006, the vision of the team that I led was to make Mauritius an ICT-focused nation and an effective bridge between ICT-advanced India and ICT-lagging Africa. The objective was to produce a large number of ICT professionals. The goal was to train and certify 400,000 Mauritians, one-third of the nation's population, in digital literacy. Six years later, Mauritius is well on its way to achieving its goal, objective and vision.

Always set high goals. I used to advise the gifted tennis teens at my academy in Florida to aim to become world champions and then work hard and smart to get there. Three of them, Andre Agassi, Monica Seles and Jim Courier, did become world champions. As Michelangelo said, "The greatest danger for most of us is not that our aim is too high and we miss it, but that it is too low and we hit it."

Setting goals with a real timeline is very important. It forces you to utilise your time, skills, money and other resources effectively to meet your goals. Remember you have exactly the same number of hours a day as Mahatma Gandhi, Mother Teresa, Abraham Lincoln and Albert Einstein. Time is a very important and finite resource. Make the most of it.

## PATHWAY

Pathway consists of the series of steps you take to get to your purpose. If you decide to go to Delhi from Mumbai, you need to decide on the path to get there. You need to specify clearly the tasks to be performed and the milestones to be accomplished along the way. Responsibility for each task should be assigned to yourself and others involved. Make sure all involved work together as a cohesive team to achieve the stated purpose including specific goals.

Recently, in providing a million poor students in America access to free Web-based online math homework help, we created a specific pathway that included emailing information to all the qualifying schools, awarding grants to them, setting up virtual CyberLearning Academies and populating them with the math homework helper programme.

It is interesting to note what is said about developing mental pathways: "As a single footstep will not make a path on the earth, so a single thought will not make a pathway in the mind. To make a deep physical path, we walk again and again. To make a deep mental path, we must think over and over the kind of thoughts we wish to dominate our lives."

## PASSION

To manage the pathway effectively to achieve your purpose, you need passion. Passion is the fuel that fires the rocket to its destination—the vision.

To succeed in life, you need passion for things you do. Passion ignites the fire in you. Passion brings out the single-minded focus to your purpose. Passion makes the pathway easier to navigate. When you discover your passion, the impossible becomes possible.

It is often said that passion is necessary for all creative endeavours. Without passion, talent cannot bloom. Albert Einstein said, "I have no special talents; I am only passionately curious." Applying passion and vision to business leaders, former Chairman of General Electric, Jack Welch, had this to say: "Good business leaders create a vision, articulate the vision, passionately own the vision, and relentlessly drive it to completion."

Apple founder and CEO Steve Jobs famously stated to his staff, "Marketing is about values. This is a very complicated world. It's a very noisy world. We're not going to get a chance for people to remember a lot about us. So, we have to be really clear about what we want them to know about us. Our customers want to know what we stand for. What we're about is not making boxes for people to get their jobs done. Although we do that very well, Apple is about more than that. We believe that people with passion can change the world for the better. That's what we believe."

Recently, in my effort to bridge the digital and employment divides in India, I created the vision of training a million disadvantaged students and jobseekers in information technology, project management and soft skills I have passionately owned the vision, and articulated it to national, state, business, academic and government leaders of India.

Passion, in effect, is an essential ingredient of your success. It is like the wind that propels your vessel. Passion ensures that your energy, time, talent and other resources are optimally employed to take you to your purpose via a smooth pathway.

## PERSEVERANCE

To get to your purpose via an effective pathway with passion, you need perseverance—commitment, resilience, smart and hard work. Perseverance is the ability to overcome difficulties by trying again and again and steadfastly adhering to a purpose and a course of action.

When someone tells me that somebody got lucky, my response is, "The smarter and harder you work, the luckier you get." The chance of a door opening is much higher if you knock on one hundred doors, rather than just one door. The very next door could be the one that opens.

Your persistence is your measure of faith in yourself. When I spoke with President Bill Clinton in 1993 and stated that I wanted to train a million poor American students in math, science and technology, I knew I would face numerous challenges. But I persisted and achieved the goal three years ahead of our target date.

Albert Einstein said, "It's not that I'm so smart, it's just that I stay with problems longer." Perseverance makes all things possible. Remember, there are obstacles in every path. The key to success is to be persistent, and turn obstacles into opportunities. A rock in your path can be used as a stepping stone. To the persistent, failure is not an option. Think of failure as a learning opportunity and a stepping stone to success. Persist, and you shall succeed in reaching your goal. Never, never give up. Remember, the darkest hour is before the dawn. The next hurdle could be your last hurdle! So, persist, and you shall succeed.

## POSITIVITY

Positivity, comprising positive attitude and positive thinking, will help you navigate your pathway to purpose with passion and perseverance.

Positivity focuses your mind on optimistic outcomes. The key to positivity is to become a positive person in thought, word and deed, so that your subconscious mind gets trained to be positive. Many great people attribute their successes to positivity.

When I helped reform the social security and healthcare system in Venezuela, we encountered several obstacles from vested-interest groups opposed to reform. Instead of panicking, I stayed positive and completed the task at hand diligently, to the delight of the Venezuelan government officials and the dismay of the reform opponents.

According to the Dalai Lama, "Having a sense of caring, a feeling of compassion will bring happiness of peace of mind to oneself, and automatically create a positive atmosphere."

Winston Churchill once said, "The optimist sees opportunity in every danger; the pessimist sees danger in every opportunity."

You have heard the common expression that an optimist will tell you the glass is half full; the pessimist, half empty. Positivity helps to convert negative stress into positive action, and fosters creativity, hope and confidence which, in turn, leads to happiness and success.

For an executive, it is important to not only think positive, but also be surrounded by positive people.

## PATIENCE

You may have heard many times the expression that patience is a virtue. As you navigate your pathway to purpose with passion, perseverance and positivity, you need patience when things get tough. Patience is defined as good-natured tolerance, the will or ability to wait or endure with steadfastness, without giving up.

When various stakeholders in Venezuela—government, business, labour and medics—delayed decisions in order to protect their vested interests, I waited patiently until I could bring all parties together to agree on a set of common goals, acceptable to all, for improving social security and healthcare.

Isaac Newton once said, "If I have ever made any valuable discoveries, it has owed more to patient attention, than to any other talent." According to *Bhagavad Gita*, "Little by little, through patience and repeated effort, the mind will become stilled in the Self."

Patience is essential to overcome obstacles on the pathway. It will help you achieve your goals. Like time, patience is a great resource to accomplish your purpose.

## PRINCIPLES

Even if you lay down a pathway to achieve your purpose with passion, perseverance, positivity and patience, you need to adhere to principles to achieve success. Case in point—a major reason for the recent global recession is the lack of principles and ethics on the part of many U.S. and global financial leaders.

Principles mean being guided by the sense of the requirements and obligations of the right conduct, based on sound moral and ethical practices.

While I was informally advising Mr. Rajiv Gandhi in 1980, I was approached by many business executives requesting that I recommend their projects to Mr. Gandhi. I told them to write a summary of the project highlighting how the project will benefit India and its people—my guiding principle in that regard. Surprise, surprise, no one ever came back to me.

It is important to live up to your principles steadfastly with conviction, especially these days when people are enamoured by money. As Tolstoy suggested, "It is easier to produce ten volumes of philosophical writing, than to put one principle into practice." In the words of Jawaharlal Nehru, India's first Prime Minister, "Failure comes only when we forget our ideals and objectives and principles." Two famous American Presidents, Thomas Jefferson and Abraham Lincoln, both advised American leaders to "stand like a rock," in matters of principles.

Making the right decisions based on sound principles, encompassing high ethical and moral values, will lead you to success and happiness.

In summary, these Seven "P's" provide you with a practical road map to success and happiness.

# CHAPTER 7

## TEN TIPS
## FOR HAPPY LIVING

*"One of the reasons I wanted to write this book is to share the happiness I have felt all along as a result of putting my beliefs into practice."*

## THE HAPPY LIVING TIPS

Let us now summarise the practice of happy living tips as they apply to executives and non-executives alike:

- **Nurture your Mind** by thinking positively and creatively. Enjoy doing so. When you see a problem, think of it as an opportunity to come up with a creative solution. Creativity leads to innovation. Think differently, look outside of your experiences for fresh ideas, and fill your brain with positive and creative thoughts and visions. I guarantee you will have fun doing so.

- **Nurture your Body** by eating healthy foods low in salt, sugar and saturated fat and zero trans-fat, and doing enjoyable physical activities, workouts, and exercises. The key is to enjoy both—eating healthy and doing physical activities.

- **Nurture your Soul** by nurturing other souls, acting in a kind, compassionate, loving, forgiving, caring and helpful manner with everyone you come across. You will discover that, by nurturing others, you are also nurturing yourself.

- **Perform activities leading to Mind-Body-Soul balance—** activities such as deep controlled breathing, meditation, yoga, visualisation, sleeping, singing, smiling and laughing. These activities also help to reduce stress. You can do these activities at your convenience daily. Performing these activities regularly will lead to peace and happiness.

- **Practise Mind-Body-Soul nurturing** in thought, word and deed: Positive thoughts lead to positive words and positive deeds. Work to create a balance within yourself and in your environment with your thoughts, words and deeds.

- **Live in the moment.** Remember, the past is gone, the future is unknown, and all we have is the present. Learn from the past, be mindful that the decisions you make today determine your happiness today, tomorrow and in the future. Make the most of your present moment by being nurturing towards yourself and others. Then the next moment will be better, and so on. Think of every moment as a gift, and celebrate it. Create a plan for the future by being mindfully aware. You can always change your plan, but you are more likely to accomplish a well thought-out plan than by having no plan at all!

- **Live for a cause larger than yourself.** As the famous Jewish philosopher Rabbi Hillel said, "If I am not for myself, who will be for me; If I am only for myself, what am I; If not now, when?" We must enjoy giving back and helping each other and it is a surprising fact that those who do so are happier than those who don't.

- **Set goals, objectives, visions and missions: Be a systems thinker.** Look at everything as a system with specific goals and objectives, and limited resources—human, financial, information, technology, physical, material and time. Always set achievable high goals and objectives, both personal and professional, whether they are daily, weekly, monthly, yearly or multi-year. Then enjoy working towards achieving them, by creating effective systems, and constantly employing the Seven "P's" for success—Purpose, Pathway, Passion, Perseverance, Positivity, Patience and Principles. Once you define clearly your purpose, including vision, mission, objectives and goals, set a clear pathway to achieve them. Practice passion, perseverance, positivity and patience as you and/your team move steadily towards your purpose. Stick to your principles all the time. This is a sure path to success and happiness.

- **Use your resources effectively.** Use all available resources systematically to achieve your visions, goals and objectives. These resources are human, financial, information, technology, physical, material and time. Time is the only equaliser for all humans; so use your time mindfully and wisely. Remember, once the minutes, hours and days are gone, they are gone forever. Find a personal and career path that makes use of your passion and your skills and interests.

- **Remember, practice makes you better.** It is good to know the concepts, but it is essential to put them into practice to get results. Phase in the practice at your comfort level. The more you practise, the more you will enjoy the activities and the happier you will be!

One of the reasons I wanted to write this book is to share the happiness I have felt all along as a result of putting my beliefs into practice. I feel happy as I am able to nurture my mind, body and soul, and connect with people with kindness and compassion on a daily basis. Thus, remember true happiness comes from nurturing the mind, body and soul of yourself and of all those you touch.

**Celebrate life, enjoy every moment, smile, laugh and BE HAPPY!**

# CHAPTER 8

## HAPPY
## EXECUTIVE
## QUIZ

*"Answer truthfully for your own benefit and to keep yourself focused on happiness."*

Think of this as a useful, fun activity to help keep you focused on happiness and creating more happiness. Answer truthfully for your own benefit. Rate each question on a scale of 1 to 5 (1 = never, 2 = once in a while, 3 = about half the time, 4 = most of the time, 5 = always).

1. Do I think positively? _____

2. Do I think creatively? _____

3. Do I eat healthy? _____ (minimum intake of salt, sugar and saturated fat; no trans fat.)

4. Do I keep my weight within the healthy range?_____(Measure your waistline at the belly button. If your waist circumference is more than half your height, you are overweight)

5. Do I perform physical activities? _____ (You get a 5, if you do physical activities at least 5 days a week, 30 minutes or more a day, amounting to 150 minutes a week. You get a 4, if you do physical activities at least 4 days a week for 30 minutes or more a day. You get a 3 for 3 days of physical activities for at least 30 minutes per day. You get a 2 for 2 days of physical activities for at least 30 minutes per day. You get a 1 for 1 day of physical activities a week for at least 30 minutes.)

6. Am I getting 7 hours of sleep each night? _____

7. Do I perform activities every day aimed at releasing/reducing stress? _____

8. Do I nurture the souls of my family, friends, co-workers and others by being loving, compassionate and caring? _____

9. Do I set a clear Purpose (including visions, objectives and goals) in my personal and professional undertakings? _____

10. Do I set a clear Pathway to achieve my purpose? _____

11. Do I bring Passion to achieve my purpose? _____

12. Do I bring Perseverance to achieve my purpose? _____

13. Do I bring Positivity to achieve my purpose? _____

14. Do I bring Patience to achieve my purpose? _____

15. Do I stick to my Principles to achieve my purpose? _____

**Total score:** _____

<u>**Grade:**</u>

Your level of Happiness, depending on your total score is:

**60-75: Excellent.**

**50-59: Good**

**40-49: Fair.**

**39 and Under**: Needs work with discipline, preceded by reflective thinking, planning, goal-setting and lifestyle changes.

## Message to the reader:

Thank you for reading Part I of this *Happy Executives* book. Please visit my websites, www.appuji.org and www.happyexecutive.org for more motivational messages, practical suggestions and updates. Enjoy a happier and healthier life every day!

—Dr. Appu Kuttan

# PART II:

## HOW I DEVELOPED MY SYSTEMS APPROACH

# CHAPTER 9

## MY EARLY
## YEARS IN INDIA

*"To ensure the best athletic and academic performance during the school year, I studied the assigned books for the next year during my summer vacation. As a result, class work was mostly review for me, and I was able to spend more time developing my football and athletic skills."*

## EARLY LIFE

I was born in 1941 in Quilon (now known as Kollam), a coastal town in the state of Kerala, India. I was the fourth of five children. Both my parents were self-starters, who pulled themselves up by their bootstraps.

My mother, orphaned at a very young age, transformed herself into an educated, teacher-turned-physician. She taught me the mental and physical gains found through yoga and meditation. I remember reading with her by the light of a kerosene lamp in the evening during my elementary school years as she emphasised the importance of academic excellence.

My father, a renowned football player and athletics champion, was an officer in the state forest department. He introduced me to a daily morning exercise routine and encouraged my participation in football and athletics, with a focus on sprinting.

Thanks to my parents, from early on, I adopted a lifestyle that included yoga, meditation and physical workout before breakfast. I have always enjoyed doing this, and have done this every day of my life including when I am travelling—in hotels, planes and ships! To this day, the daily morning routine really invigorates me, preparing me to face the day's work and challenges with a healthy body, positive attitude, a clear mind and compassionate spirit.

## MY FATHER

My father gave me one very important piece of advice that has always stuck in my mind. In the 1920s, during competitions between the British Army in India and the Indian Stars team, my father won the athletics championship and scored the winning goal in the football match. The British commander, who was a real sports enthusiast, offered my father a commission in the army, a rare offer for a young Indian college student in those days.

Having no one in his family to advise him on such matters, my father turned to his principal, an Englishman at St. Joseph's College, Trichy, for guidance. The principal, to keep his star athlete in college for another year, advised my father to turn down the commander's offer. "You can inform the commander that you will accept his offer next year," the principal told my father.

My father followed his advice. The next year, the Commander had returned to England and the new Commander who took over had no interest in sports. My father was very disappointed. After all, if he had accepted the commission, he would have probably become the Commander-in-Chief of the Indian Army. Instead, he retired as a mid-level government official.

"When you see a unique opportunity, seize it; you may never get it again," my father told me. Later I learned there is a Latin phrase that contains similar words, "carpe diem," which means seize the day. It is a very old and sage bit of wisdom which has served me well throughout my career. My unassuming father was my athletics hero and role model.

## MY MOTHER

My mother, a physician, was the hardest worker I have ever known. As a child, I saw her wake up at night and go out numerous times to help pregnant women with their deliveries, having done the same throughout the day at the hospital. There were not many paved roads or cars in those days. During the monsoons, it was very difficult riding in a rickshaw with the wheels often getting stuck in mud. Yet, she was constantly in motion.

My mother taught me, by example, that the smarter and harder you work, the luckier you get. She was not afraid to seek opportunities. As a young girl, she walked barefoot several miles along the rail tracks to attend the convent school in the town of Quilon. As a teacher, on her own initiative, she wrote to the Maharaja of Travancore asking for a scholarship to study medicine to provide a needed service to the people—something no one had dared to do in those days. Her caring, compassionate, spiritual nature, even while under the stress of delivering babies of poor parents, often in huts at night without electricity, constantly reminded me that I could overcome all obstacles. My mother was my academic, professional and spiritual role model.

## MY SCHOOL YEARS

When I was six years old, Mahatma Gandhi was assassinated, and on that day I vividly remember going with my grandmother to the temple to offer prayers.

When I turned 14, I developed a keen interest in the Mahatma's writings and spent a whole summer vacation reading every book I could find to teach myself about his life, ideas and accomplishments. I was profoundly influenced by his thinking and his ability to develop and apply simple practical concepts by garnering the support of millions of Indians. His work taught me the importance of the Four "P's" — Principles, Passion, Perseverance and Patience. His words, "a man is but the product of his thoughts; what he thinks, he becomes," and "the best way to find yourself is to lose yourself in the service of others," along with the influence of my parents as role models, planted in me the seeds of the happy executive concept and lifestyle.

From early on, I studied hard to become a top student and practised hard to become a top football player and athlete. I liked the challenge of staying on top in the academic and athletic arenas and, on my own, I devised an effective time-management system to do so.

To ensure the best athletic and academic performance during the school year, I studied the assigned books for the next year during my summer vacation. As a result, class work was mostly review for me, and I was able to spend more time developing my football and athletic skills.

While in college, I also had an opportunity to train with the world-renowned German athletics coach, Dr. Otto Peltzer.

I studied electrical engineering at Trivandrum Engineering College of the populous Kerala University and, by the time I graduated in 1963, I had become an accomplished university athletics champion and team captain, an important member of the football team, and a top student—a rare feat in India, where top students study all the time, and top athletes mostly play.

It was at the engineering college that I first conceived the concept of systems thinking—using resources effectively to meet objectives and goals. In my third year, the college was moved to a location several miles outside the city. In the new location, there were no athletic facilities. As a result, I, along with other members of the football and athletics teams, had to travel for hours by bus to the city to practise. When I confronted the principal about this problem, he told me nothing could be done apart from waiting for a stadium to be built, maybe in a few years. Instead of being discouraged, I hired workers with funds I collected from my parents and fellow students. Then, during a two-week vacation, I created a football field with less than 250 Rupees. This football field remained the primary playing field for the college for many years. Carpe diem!

## WORKING IN BOMBAY

In 1963, I went to Bombay, now known as Mumbai, to join a Tata company. Soon, however, I found out about a new management training programme at Larsen & Toubro, a progressive Danish engineering company. I applied and was selected as the first management trainee. I developed a special relationship with the Danish manager, Bjorn Petersen, who encouraged me to use creative solutions by thinking out of the box. Independently, I studied industrial engineering books and helped to reduce significantly the switchboard assembly time by designing and implementing a new system.

I continued my athletics training, making time in my busy schedule by taking a 5:00 a.m. train to the city to train with the national athletics coach, Ullal Rao, and then arriving at work promptly at 8:00 a.m. I won the sprint events in some of the athletic meets in Bombay.

The experience in Bombay taught me to be very goal-oriented in my professional life.

Appu Kuttan's high school photo in the National Cadet Corps uniform.

Dr. Appu Kuttan's father Narayanan Palpu (sitting left most) with his college football teammates at the St. Joseph's College in Trichy, Tamil Nadu. His bare-footed Indian national team beat the British Army team.

College student Appu Kuttan with his father and three brothers with their athletic and football trophies. From left to right: Appu Kuttan, P. Balakrishnan, P. Gopinathan, Narayanan Palpu and Chandra Sekhar.

Appu Kuttan on the medal stand for the 100 meters winners at the Kerala University Athletic meet in 1962-63.

Appu Kuttan winning the 200 meters sprint by a wide margin at the Kerala University Athletic Meet.

Appu Kuttan crowned as the 1962-63 Kerala University athletic champion. He won both the 100 meters and 200 meters sprint races, was runner up in long jump, and also led the Trivandrum College of Engineering team to wins in both the 4x100 and 4x400 relay events. He single-handedly helped the Engineering College win the championship for the first time in many years.

Appu Kuttan taking the oath as captain of the Kerala University team at the 1962-63 Indian National Universities Athletic Meet in Punjab.

Appu Kuttan winning the 200 meters sprint event at an Athletic Meet in Bombay. He went on to win the 100 meters and long jump, and was crowned the overall champion.

# CHAPTER 10

## GRADUATE STUDIES AND CONTRIBUTIONS TO THE UNITED STATES, INDIA AND OTHER COUNTRIES

*"I often pose a question, "What is the one source that is both capitalist and socialist?" Often I get responses from CEOs that there cannot be such a source, since capitalism and socialism are mutually exclusive concepts. To which I respond, "The answer is God. God is both a capitalist and a socialist.*

*God gives us all 24 hours a day, irrespective of our differences—this is a socialistic concept. Then God says what we do with our 24 hours a day decides how healthy, happy and wealthy we are—a capitalistic concept."*

## GRADUATE STUDIES IN THE UNITED STATES

In 1964, I received the prestigious and coveted Tata Scholarship, similar to the Rhodes scholarship awarded in the United States, so I could pursue graduate studies in the United States. I was one of only 50 Tata scholars chosen from all over India that year. I was also awarded a scholarship to study industrial engineering at Washington University in St. Louis, Missouri, by Professor Gerald Nadler, a renowned work systems professor who was impressed by a paper I sent him about my switchboard assembly work at Larsen & Toubro. Before our departure to the United States, the wise octogenarian Tata Foundation director said to us, the Tata scholars, "You are our ambassadors. The impression Americans will form about India and Indians will depend on you and how you behave. Always be polite, tip well, dress well, speak well, and act well."

In those days, the Tata Foundation insisted on travel to the United States by ship, believing that sea travel would help its scholars grow accustomed to the Western lifestyle, food, customs and people. The first leg from Bombay to London was my first ever experience of travelling on a ship, and I was exposed to the choppiness of the Arabian Sea. As the least affected, I was able to help care for my seasick fellow scholars. By the time we arrived in London, we were relieved and ready to set foot on land. However, our time in London was short, and we found ourselves back on board a bigger ship to New York after just two days.

The journey to New York was more interesting and pleasant. I won Ping-Pong and crossword puzzle competitions and engaged in serious thought-provoking discussions about God with a group of Catholic priests. I was able to have them accept my strong belief that God is consciousness, truth and omnipresence, and that divinity is manifested in everyone.

Through kindness and compassion in thought, word, and deed, we honour and nurture that divinity.

I remember the excitement at the first sighting of the imposing 305-foot Statue of Liberty at dawn as we entered the New York Harbour. I learned that the statue was a gift from France in 1886 and it had come to symbolise the line from Emma Lazarus's poem, *The New Colossus*— "Give me your tired, your poor, your huddled masses yearning to breathe free"— turning Liberty into a welcoming mother, a symbol of hope. I was awe-struck by the New York skyscrapers and spent a few days in the city before travelling by bus to Washington University in St. Louis.

The first day I arrived at the freezing bus station in St. Louis, I was met by an Indian graduate fellow who had luckily thought ahead and brought me a coat. When I got off the bus, I saw snow for the first time. Coming from India, I had no winter clothes. It was quite an exhilarating experience, and a few weeks later I found myself walking through three feet of snow!

## MASTERS AT WASHINGTON UNIVERSITY

When I went to Washington University in St. Louis, Missouri, I learned Professor Nadler had moved to the University of Wisconsin to become chairman of the industrial engineering department. Because I had anticipated working with him, I called him for guidance and he suggested I finish my Masters at Washington University and then come to Wisconsin for a Doctorate. He said he could offer me a scholarship for the next year.

I told my graduate advisor I wanted to finish my Masters in two semesters, about 10 months, so I could join Professor Nadler by the summer of 1965. He reluctantly consented. I ended up taking 18 graduate credits and auditing nine undergraduate credits in the first semester, since I was now switching my major from Electrical Engineering to Industrial Engineering. I was in class all day long and did my work in my campus office all night until four in the morning.

It is worth pointing out an interesting experience I had relating to honesty. While walking home from my campus office during the early morning hours, I was struck by the honesty of the residents living in the vicinity of the university campus. I saw empty milk bottles with dollar bills on the front step of the row houses. I also had professors who asked us to take the final closed book exams at home within the prescribed time. I cannot imagine such things happening these days in America or anywhere else; America and the world have changed!

## DOCTORATE AT THE UNIVERSITY OF WISCONSIN AND THE CREATION OF MBS

As I had planned, I received my Masters in the summer of 1965 and moved to Madison, Wisconsin, to pursue my Doctorate studies with Professor Nadler. The first thing I noticed in Madison was the presence of a relatively large Indian student population on the famously liberal Midwest campus.

In 1968, I completed my doctorate in Industrial Engineering, with majors in systems engineering, human factors engineering, behaviour cybernetics, statistics and management. I developed the **Management By Systems (MBS)** concept the same year.

MBS is essentially a systems approach to management. It begins with defining clearly the visions, missions, goals and objectives of an organisation/programme by an executive or a team. Then the team maps the existing available resources, namely, human, financial, information, technology, physical, material and time. This is followed by an assessment of additional resources required to achieve the defined goals and objectives, development of creative and outside the box thinking solutions, prioritisation of the solutions, development of an implementation plan, implementation, monitoring and continuous improvement. MBS can be applied to any programme or system ranging from a work station to a nation, since all are systems. Everyone from the President/Prime Minister of a nation to a worker in an office or a factory is a systems person, trying to set objectives and goals, whether daily, weekly, monthly, yearly or longer term, and then trying to use available resources effectively to achieve them.

**In summary, MBS is a way of thinking—always establishing specific goals and objectives, and then finding the most innovative and cost-effective ways of using all available resources to achieve them by creating a system.**

A more detailed discussion of the MBS way of thinking can be found at www.cyberlearning.org/mbs.

Regarding resources, it is worth noting that even though financial resources are important, the human resource is the most important of all resources in any system, because humans make decisions about the deployment of all other resources. And when I talk about time as a resource to audiences, I often pose a question, "What is the one source that is both capitalist and socialist?" Often I get responses from CEOs that there cannot be such a source, since capitalism and socialism are mutually exclusive concepts. To which I respond, "The answer is God. God is both a capitalist and a socialist. God gives us all 24 hours a day, irrespective of our differences—this is a socialistic concept. Then God says what we do with our 24 hours a day decides how healthy, happy and wealthy we are—a capitalistic concept."

While at the University of Wisconsin, I remember expressing in a business class, my strong view that business ethics should be taught in all MBA programmes. The US and global financial upheaval of the last few years, caused by unethical and greedy practices of financial executives, has convinced me that MBA students should be required to take a Professional Business License Exam, much like doctors and lawyers, and ethics should be an important part of that exam.

## MY WIFE AND MY FAMILY

I met my wife, Claudia, a Wisconsin native, in Madison in 1965 at a University of Wisconsin open lecture. She switched from studying the sciences on a National Science Foundation scholarship to studying Journalism and Mass Communications, thinking that would be quicker to complete and more useful for us. She also took courses in the social sciences and undergrad and graduate courses on India so she could better understand me and my culture. In addition, she undertook post graduate courses in Survey Research and Reference Research.

We were married in 1967. Claudia has been the anchor in my life. Claudia comes from a family with tremendous mental fortitude. She was taught not only to be positive and kind, but that every day is a blessing. She was told that she could do anything she set her mind to do, that there are many ways to solve problems, to never give up, and to check and verify everything. Her family taught her to stand for what she believed in. She regards reading and learning as lifelong activities. One summer, while our son Roger was taking courses at Stanford, Claudia enrolled our daughter, Maya, in various programmes for children taking place on campus. Claudia also enrolled herself in a course entitled, "Critical Thinking and Creative Problem Solving." The class was open to all undergrad and grad students as well as to the faculty. Bill Gates was among the guest speakers. Claudia is a voracious reader and a lifelong learner.

If anyone asks Claudia what she does, her response is always, "Being a mom," besides "Helping my husband." She considers being "mom" her most important responsibility and her privilege and honor. There is a tradition in her family to teach and provide the children with everything that was taught and provided to them, and then to build on that.

We have been married for 46 years, and have been blessed with two wonderful children, Roger (Raj) and Maya.

Roger was honoured by President Bill Clinton during the US Presidential Inauguration in 1993 as a "Face of Hope," for young Americans. At that time, 19-year-old Roger was the youngest university valedictorian in the United States, a Wall Street money manager, and Volvo Tennis Scholar-Athlete All-American Award winner. At the invitation of President Clinton, Roger, Maya, Claudia and I attended several evening balls and the week-long inaugural events with front row seats. We also were treated to a private tour of the White House. Roger went on to earn a Juris Doctor (J.D) in law and an M.B.A in business from Stanford University, with specialties in investment, global management and public management. He is currently serving as Vice President of our National Education Foundation, and also continues to manage investments for a select group of family and friends.

Maya is an award-winning filmmaker and environmentalist. Maya earned a J.D. from the University of California Los Angeles (UCLA) School of Law, with a focus on public interest environmental law, and a Bachelor of Arts degree from the University of Southern California's School of Cinematic Arts. At UCLA, Maya was president of the Environmental Law Society, and Chief Articles Editor for the Journal of Environmental Law & Policy. As a member of UCLA's delegation to the 2009 United Nations Climate Change Conference in Copenhagen, she met with key U.S. and Indian negotiators and Nobel Laureate Dr. Rajendra Pachauri. Maya has honed her skills in environmental law through her work at the Natural Resources Section of the California Attorney General's Office, the Natural Resources Defense Council (NRDC) and the US Environmental Protection Agency (EPA).

My wife often jokes that in a previous life she was probably born in India, since she loves Indian food, philosophy, and culture so much! I say that I went to the University of Wisconsin and got both my doctorate and my wife. The unconditional love and support of my family have been fundamental to all my activities and accomplishments over the years.

## IMPROVING HIGHER EDUCATION AND TRAFFIC SAFETY IN PUERTO RICO

Upon receiving my doctorate, I was offered many interesting jobs, including professorships at prestigious universities, executive positions at major corporations and the coveted Human Factors Engineer position at NASA, the United States Space Agency, to simulate spacemen—a job requiring immediate security clearance. Even though these offers were very attractive, I decided to take the job as a professor at the University of Puerto Rico at a much lower salary than the other offers. I felt Puerto Rico, as a United State territory, with both developed and developing areas, would provide me a unique opportunity to apply my MBS concept to socio-economic problems—a dream of mine influenced by my studies of Mahatma Gandhi during my school days in India.

I arrived in Puerto Rico in the fall of 1968. I had to quickly learn conversational Spanish, the native language. Fortunately, because the textbooks were in English and the students understood English, I did not have to teach my classes in Spanish.

During my first year at the University of Puerto Rico, I was able to help the Industrial Engineering Department get full United States accreditation by applying the MBS approach—they had been trying to get accredited for many years prior to my arrival with no success. I was also chosen as the Professor of the Year by the students. Thus, my first year out of my doctoral programme was quite hectic, yet rewarding.

The following year, I was offered a full professorship at the University's Business School to help set up its M.B.A programme. I was told that I was one of the youngest full professors in the United States at that time.

I often told my students that getting a college degree is like getting a driver's license. It is what you do after you get your degree that truly determines if you really deserve the degree. The degree is not the end achievement, but the beginning of what you can achieve. Thus I exhorted my students to work smart and hard after graduation to achieve specific personal and professional goals and objectives.

In early 1970, the Government of Puerto Rico invited me to tackle its serious traffic safety problem—Puerto Rico's traffic fatality rate was more than twice the rate in the United States. This was the opportunity I had been waiting for—the chance to apply MBS (**Management By Systems**) to improve socio-economic programmes.

First, I put together a team of traffic safety experts and organised the traffic safety system into 24 subsystems ranging from driver education to drunk driving. I then hired 24 graduate students and trained them in MBS. We set up 24 teams, one for each subsystem, comprising leaders from the community, government, education, religious groups and public and private sectors.

I said to Governor Luis Ferre up front that we have to make it a project of the people to gain legislative support for the implementation of the measures. Accordingly, we proceeded to conduct an ideas contest through television, radio and the press. We asked the people of Puerto Rico to write to us their ideas on how to improve one or more of the subsystems. We offered attractive prizes for winners. We received over 18,000 entries! The winner, a veteran traffic judge, submitted 160 pages of ideas and won the first prize—an all-expense-paid round-trip to Paris for two! We also solicited ideas from traffic safety experts around the world and distributed them to the 24 teams, asking them to come up with the best, most cost-effective solutions.

These subsystem solutions were then integrated by our team to provide 30 different system solutions. We selected 10 high-priority solutions and presented them to the administrative, legislative, judicial and community leaders in a public function presided over by the Governor. The legislature made changes to the laws, such as reducing the blood alcohol level for drivers. We then developed an MBS implementation plan and put the programme into action including alcohol patrols on the roads. The result: traffic fatalities were reduced by 20% in just the first year alone!

## CHALLENGES IN VENEZUELA

Based on my success in Puerto Rico, the Government of Venezuela invited me in 1975 to tackle their serious social security and healthcare problems. Their social security program, which also provided national healthcare, had a budget larger than most of the other government agency budgets combined. President Carlos Andres Perez had recently won the election on the promise that he would reform the unmanageable social security system and he made it a high priority for his administration and the nation, since social security and healthcare services affected the lives of most people.

Upon my arrival in Caracas, the capital of Venezuela, I soon found that very few people spoke English. Hence, I conducted all my business in Spanish. During my first meeting with the national leaders, the atmosphere was gloomy indeed, but the participants appreciated my effort to communicate with them in Spanish. They were also grateful for my frank comment that I was there only as a catalyst to help them to think out-of-the-box, so that they could come up with appropriate and creative cost-effective solutions to their urgent problems.

My initial daytime meetings with stakeholder's leaders—government, labour unions, chamber of commerce and the medical association—were not fruitful because their advisors quickly shot down any new ideas that were brought up. To effectively involve the stakeholders and devise new plans, I then invited all the key decision-makers without their advisors for frequent dinner meetings at the Caracas Hilton, where I was put up by the government. I realised that the key to success was bringing all the leaders of the stakeholder organisations together from the very beginning and making it their project, engaging them in consensus building from the goal-setting phase to the implementation and monitoring phases.

Just days into the project, I was told that IBM had presented a multi-million dollar proposal to create a modern management information system over a multi-year period. I told the stakeholders that by the time the new IBM system would come through, social security would be bankrupt, and so it was not a viable solution.

We analysed social security as a system and set an initial goal to collect millions of dollars from accounts that had remained outstanding for several months. I was astounded to see that their billing was behind by six months. We promptly proceeded to create six teams, including IT professionals I brought from the United States and India. Each team updated the invoicing for one month by working on weekends at the idle government agency computer centres. Thus, in less than six weeks, we updated the invoicing system and sent out bills—warning companies and other organisations to pay up or face the cut off of services. As a result, social security was able to collect millions of dollars, and that allowed us to reform the various pension and healthcare service programmes.

Another serious problem our team faced was older people waiting in lines for hours outdoors, in all kinds of weather, to collect monthly pension cheques at the pension payment offices. The bureaucratic solution the government officials came up with was to increase the number of offices at a cost of several million dollars. The final creative solution our team came up with was to distribute the pension funds through the banks. This resulted in the elimination of people waiting in long queues, often outdoors in inclement weather, at all the pension payment offices. An unexpected bonus was a significant reduction in pension payments, because banks, unlike the offices, gave pension cheques only to people with proper identification!

The results of the social security reforms were phenomenal. In three years, we were able to transform the National Social Security Program from a deficit to a surplus operation, changing the information and invoicing systems, as well as the sick leave and pension payment systems while improving the quality of service.

Initially, I took my wife and our three-year-old son with me from our family home in metro Washington, D.C., to my suite at the Caracas Hilton. There we had unique opportunities to meet, dine and play tennis with many visiting celebrities including the famous American singer, Michael Jackson. But as I started getting anonymous threats because of the social security reforms, I had to send my family back to Washington, D.C. I stayed on and saw the project through implementation, since I believed that the project presented me with a unique and rare opportunity to help make a difference in the lives of millions of Venezuelans.

For me, the three years in Venezuela were like a lifetime filled with all kinds of challenging experiences. Of course, life in Puerto Rico had prepared me to deal with the Latin "mañana" (tomorrow) culture that says "What can be done today can be done tomorrow, so no need to hurry today." The people were very friendly to me, especially since I spoke fluent Spanish. They really enjoy life. In Venezuela, they say "cheers" by raising glasses and saying, "salud, amor y dinero,"—meaning health, love and money in that order. The Venezuelans often joked that the Americans had their priorities reversed—make money first and then seek love and health! I really enjoyed the Venezuelan people, culture, music and food.

I remember when a profile article headlined, ***"Wizard from India fixes Venezuela's Social Security,"*** was published in ***Zeta***, a major Venezuelan publication, the Indian Ambassador in Venezuela thanked me for helping to build an excellent image for India and Indians in Venezuela.

## WORLD TOUR

When I completed the Venezuelan Social Security project and returned to Washington, D.C., in 1978, I told my wife and son that I was going to take the next few months off and take them wherever they wished to go. My wife grew up in a home where they took regular family travel vacations. We undertook a world tour. On our way to India, we saw the pageantry in London, the Louvre museum and Eiffel Tower in Paris, the mountains, valleys and lakes of Switzerland, and the Coliseum and other ancient ruins in Rome.

In India, we visited my parents in lush Kerala and travelled all around the state seeing many historical places such as the Padmanabhaswamy Temple located at Trivandrum (now known as Thiruvananthapuram), the inner sanctum of which is said to be over 5,000 years old. We also visited the famous beaches of Kovalam and the Periyar Wildlife Sanctuary with its wild elephants, flying squirrels, etc.

Then, we travelled all over India visiting many historic sites and tourist attractions ranging from the awe-inspiring Taj Mahal to the surreal paintings in the Ajanta Caves. We rode an elephant to the mirrored palace in the pink city of Jaipur, visited the tree that the Buddha meditated under near Benares, and stayed on a boat on a Kashmir lake. Then on the way back, we visited Hong Kong, both the bustling city and colourful harbour; Tokyo, including the beautiful Tokyo Imperial Palace East Garden; and the tropical paradise of Hawaii. It was quite an adventure for our five-year-old son and us.

## VISITING THE U.S. NATIONAL PARKS

The following summer, our son said, "Let's go to the national parks." He had become very interested in the U.S. National Parks after watching television shows about them. There are 58 of them all across the United States. I told him that I would be the driver, and that he needed to read up on the parks and be ready to ask the park rangers questions. Accordingly, my wife and I bought travel and park books for him, and helped him make a three-month travel plan.

It was Roger's first trip to the wilderness parks. The trip was filled with adventures in the immensely huge parks of natural wonders, majestic natural beauty, wild animals, ranger-led educational programmes, hikes, white river rafting, and ghost towns abandoned by miners years ago. Some of the highlights were the Mammoth Cave—the longest cave system in the world, and Yellowstone National Park, with its famous Old Faithful Geyser and several other geysers, hot springs and waterfalls. We saw over 60 wild mammals including bears, wolves, elk, buffalo, mule deer, bison, moose, bighorn sheep, mountain goat, pronghorn and white-tailed deer.

The steep and colourful Grand Canyon is the largest canyon in the world. Geologically, it is significant because nearly two billion years of the earth's geological history had been exposed on the walls of the canyon, when the Colorado River cut through layer after layer of rock. The oldest layer is the two-billion-year-old Vishnu Schist at the bottom of the Inner Gorge, named after the Hindu God, Vishnu.

At the Dinosaur National Monument, we saw countless dinosaur fossils embedded on the side of a mountain cliff inside the Quarry Visitor Centre built over that exposed cliff face. We walked down to the bottom of the Meteor Crater, the world's best preserved meteorite impact site. The Meteor Crater is the result of a collision 50,000 years ago between a piece of an asteroid travelling at 26,000 miles per hour and the planet earth! We walked along trails inside Yosemite National Park, famous for its Half Dome, and also known for its waterfalls and ancient giant sequoia trees. We also drove down the beautiful coast of California, visiting Disneyland and other places.

While driving to the parks, we played math games with the numbers on car license plates in front of us, starting with simple one and two-digit additions and other basic math, and progressing to doing two and three-digit math operations, calculating travel times and finding the largest prime numbers, etc.

When we got back to Washington, D.C., our son's teachers were amazed at the multi-level grade advancement in his reading and math skills. That experience reinforced my theory on early childhood education—help children enjoy learning as a fun activity, and let them learn by doing fun activities they enjoy. This way, they learn to love learning, thinking, and problem solving as well as math, reading, science, presentation skills and communication skills.

## GIVING BACK TO INDIA

In 1980, in my desire to give back to India, I volunteered to assist Mr. Rajiv Gandhi when he was pressed into politics by his mother, Prime Minister Indira Gandhi. In our first conversation, Mr. Gandhi was very frank. He said, in effect, that he was a pilot and that he did not know much about management or systems. He asked me what I could teach him in a weekend. I told him that I could teach him everything they teach at the Harvard Business School about strategic management. I added that, if he was being groomed to become the future Prime Minister of a billion people, he should not worry about operational management; instead, he should focus on setting a vision to help India compete in the global economy by using its resources effectively.

I taught Mr. Gandhi Management By Systems (MBS). Then he asked me to talk to top government officials in Delhi including the then Planning Commission member and the present Prime Minister of India, Manmohan Singh. After training a number of top government officials in the ensuing weeks, Mr. Gandhi and I discussed a vision to make India an IT power (Information Technology), with input from many leaders.

The rationale we laid out was simple. India was ideally suited to become an IT power for three reasons:

1. The English language, already spoken by the college graduates in India, would be the language of the coming IT age;

2. India was producing more math, science and engineering graduates than any other country, and these graduates could easily be trained in IT, since IT requires the same logical thinking skills;

3. Indians love working with computers. (I had brought a few Indian IT professionals to work with me to design and implement an information system for the Venezuelan Social Security in the 70's, and they were happy to work long hours to get the job done.)

My counsel to Mr. Gandhi was this: "When you become Prime Minister, abolish the restrictions on foreign company operations in India set by Prime Minister Mrs. Indira Gandhi, and invite technology companies to come and set up shop in India, so that they can train Indians in IT. Then, the trained Indians can work for companies and organizations all over the world."

I kept in touch with Mr. Gandhi and we spent time together when he accompanied his mother on her official trip to Washington, D.C., in the early 80s. When Mr. Gandhi became Prime Minister in 1984, he started implementing his vision to make India an IT power. The rest is history. Today, one in three IT professionals in the world is an Indian!

I only planned to stay in India for a month, but ended up staying and working as a volunteer for several months, informally advising Mr. Gandhi and teaching the MBS concept to many top government officials. On Mr. Gandhi's birthday, a couple of days before I returned to the United States, I gave him a cheque written to the Prime Minister's Relief Fund, thus donating all the funds left in my Indian bank account for a good cause.

I remember travelling with Mr. Gandhi and his wife Sonia Gandhi—currently the most powerful political person in India—to London on my way back to Washington, D.C. Mr. Gandhi and I had another long and frank discussion. When I asked him what the greatest contribution of his family to India was, he didn't blink an eye. He said it was holding India together since Independence. When he asked me what I thought about Mrs. Indira Gandhi's management style, I was equally frank. "Mrs. Gandhi is one of the most politically astute leaders in the world, but her 'crisis management' style is far less productive than the 'management by systems, visions and objectives' style. A good manager is pro-active, not reactive. I hope you will adopt the pro-active, visionary management style." He laughed and nodded!

While in Delhi, I had many interesting intellectual discussions during weekend lunch sessions with the wise Indian Supreme Court Justice V. R. Krishna Iyer, whom I had known for many years. Justice Krishna Iyer also introduced me to Dr. K. R. Narayanan, the then Vice-Chancellor of the Jawaharlal Nehru University, who later became the President of India. The venerable 96-year-old Justice Krishna Iyer, a "living legend" in the world of judiciary, has continued to send me advice. One piece of advice in early 2009 was, "You should do whatever you can to assist President Obama, since his success is essential for global peace and economic health."

While in Delhi, one idea I floated for Mr. Rajiv Gandhi was to set up a think tank of prominent overseas Indians to look into India's problems and visions from an outside perspective. Mr. Gandhi really liked the idea and arranged meetings to find the resources needed. The committee we set up did not follow through once I left Delhi, as predicted by Justice Krishna Iyer.

## BACK IN WASHINGTON, D.C.

Once I returned to Washington, D.C. from Delhi in 1980, I got involved with consulting activities and taking our son around to tennis tournaments. Meanwhile, Dr. K. R. Narayanan was appointed the Indian Ambassador to the United States. During his 1980-1984 ambassadorship, we became good friends. We had many interesting weekend lunch discussions. He told me that Mr. Rajiv Gandhi specifically requested that he arrange a private meeting with me, when Mr. Gandhi accompanied Prime Minister Indira Gandhi on her 1982 landmark visit to Washington, D.C.

Before Dr. Narayanan's ambassadorial term was coming to a close, Mrs. Usha Narayanan requested that I ask Mr. Rajiv Gandhi what plans Mrs.

Gandhi had for Dr. Narayanan upon his return to Delhi. Mr. Gandhi said, "Just tell Ambassador Narayanan not to worry. Our family has always found ways to use his extraordinary talents and will continue to do so." Upon his return, Dr. Narayanan became a Cabinet Minister, then Vice President and ultimately the President of India in 1997.

In 1981, Ambassador Narayanan and I set up the Tata Scholars Alumni Association (TSAA) in Washington, D.C. with Dr. Narayanan as the Honorary Chairman and myself as the President. The Association is being revived now and details are available at *www.tatascholars.org*.

## FORAY INTO TENNIS – PRODUCING WORLD CHAMPIONS

In 1984, our son Roger, then ten, took his first college course at the prestigious Johns Hopkins University. He was also one of the top 10 junior tennis players in the United States. He wanted to become a professional tennis player. I told him, "Your future is with your mind, but if you want to become a tennis professional, you have to go to Florida or California, and practise year-round with the best players." He really wanted to become a tennis pro, and so we moved to Florida.

Soon after, I bought the financially-floundering, world famous, Nick Bollettieri Tennis Academy. We turned the financially weak academy into a profitable business in one year.

I discovered it is possible to create world champions if you take talented kids and put them in the programme, give them all the tools and make training fun for them.

Accordingly, we applied my Management By Systems (MBS) approach, thought out-of-the-box, and created the Total Tennis System emphasising mental toughness, physical conditioning, strategy and weapon strokes—the two or three dependable strokes one can call upon at critical times. In addition, we increased the practice time for serves and returns, since every point begins with them. We also worked on improving the players' reaction times and movement time, since the information theory research I had done indicated that faster reaction and movement time contribute to improved strokes.

Then, by giving our youngsters the opportunity to play in tournaments during weekends and practice with tennis professionals we brought to the academy, we helped build their skills and self-confidence. The result was three world champions: Andre Agassi, Monica Seles and Jim Courier.

See *www.cyberlearning.org/tennis.*

While still at the tennis academy, I received a call from Mr. Rajiv Gandhi, asking if his son, Rahul, then a student at Harvard University, could come over to Florida to spend a few days with me. I gladly said yes, but the visit never took place as Mr. Rahul Gandhi's plans changed.

In 1964, Appu Kuttan was chosen as one of India's top 50 Tata Scholars for study abroad. In addition, he also received a scholarship to study Industrial Engineering at Washington University in St. Louis, USA, from World-renowned professor Gerald Nadler.

Appu Kuttan met his wife-to-be Claudia, a native of Wisconsin at the University of Wisconsin, Madison, Wisconsin, in 1965.

Claudia standing on the University of Wisconsin Campus edge by Lake Mendota, Madison, where they often picnicked and went boating.

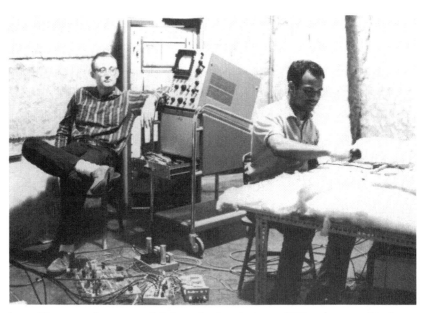

Appu Kuttan in his research lab at the University of Wisconsin in Madison, Wisconsin, in 1967.

Claudia wearing a sari at the University of Wisconsin International Fashion Show in Madison, Wisconsin, in 1965.

Appu Kuttan and Claudia on the University of Wisconsin Campus in Madison, Wisconsin, in 1966.

Appu Kuttan married Claudia in 1967 at the Unitarian Meeting House in Madison, which was designed by the World-famous architect Frank Lloyd Wright.

Appu Kuttan and Claudia with friends and family at their wedding.

Appu Kuttan and Claudia on their honeymoon.

Claudia Kuttan modeling a sari at the University of Wisconsin International
Fashion show in Madison, Wisconsin, in 1967.

Appu Kuttan and wife Claudia appeared in the ***Malayala Manorama*** newspaper while they visited family in Kerala, in 1969.

Appu Kuttan and wife Claudia standing next to a Mughal architectural masterpiece in North India, in 1969.

Appu Kuttan and wife Claudia fishing in the pristine waters in the beautiful
Kashmir valley, in 1969.

Claudia Kuttan at the Kovalam Beach in Kerala, in 1969.

Appu Kuttan and wife Claudia at the dinner celebrating the success of his traffic safety project in Puerto Rico, in 1970.

Appu Kuttan (fourth from left) and Claudia Kuttan (sixth from left) with the famous Harvard Professor John Galbraith (ninth from left) and fellow faculty members of the University of Puerto Rico Graduate School of Business in San Juan, Puerto Rico, in 1970.

**"Appu Kuttan stands where the action is"**, says a profile article entitled **"Appu Kuttan solves traffic problems in Puerto Rico."** The article was published in the August 1971 edition of the prestigious *Industrial Engineering*.

Appu Kuttan being congratulated by Luis Ferre, the Governor of Puerto Rico, in 1971, for helping to reduce Puerto Rico's traffic fatalities by 20% in just the first year.

Claudia Kuttan holding baby son Roger and her University diploma in front of the statue of Abraham Lincoln on the University of Wisconsin Campus, in 1974.

Appu Kuttan holding baby son Roger, in 1974.

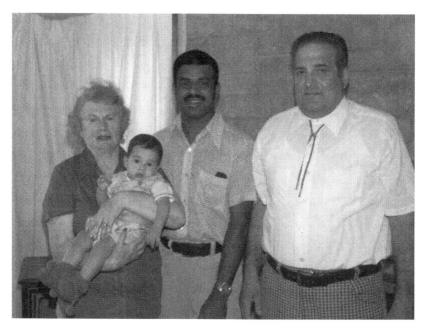

Appu Kuttan with in-laws Jean Shapiro (holding Roger) and Marvin Shapiro, a decorated World War II American hero.

Appu Kuttan and Claudia with their son Roger in Madison, Wisconsin, in 1974.

Appu Kuttan's Family photo in Washington, DC, in 1975—Appu, Roger and Claudia with Appu Kuttan's brother Chandra Sekhar, father Narayanan Palpu and mother Dr. Narayani Lakshmi.

Roger Kuttan at home in Washington, DC, with football.

Roger Kuttan standing between the snowmen he made in front of his Washington, DC, home.

Appu Kuttan holding Roger at the beautiful Luquillo Beach in Puerto Rico.

Claudia Kuttan with Roger on the historic Spanish El Morro Fort grounds in San Juan, Puerto Rico. Roger's kite is in the background.

Roger playing in the gardens of the beach-side Caribe Hilton hotel in San Juan, Puerto Rico.

World-famous singer Michael Jackson holding Roger Kuttan at the Caracas Hilton in Caracas, Venezuela, in 1975, when Appu Kuttan hosted Michael Jackson.

Appu Kuttan as he appeared in the profile article, **"Appu Kuttan—Wizard from India in Venezuela's Social Security."** The profile was published in the 1977 May edition of *ZETA*, the national news magazine of Venezuela.

Appu Kuttan holding Roger at a party congratulating him on reforming the social security and healthcare programs in Venezuela, in 1977.

Appu Kuttan holding Roger at the Guards Ceremony at Buckingham Palace in London, in 1978.

Appu Kuttan with Claudia and Roger in front of the Arc de Triomphe in Paris, in 1978.

Roger Kuttan at the Eiffel Tower in Paris, in 1978.

Appu Kuttan holding Roger in Vatican City, within Rome, in 1978. Vatican City houses St. Peter's Basilica, the Apostolic Palace, and Sistine Chapel whose ceiling painting 'The Last Judgment' is widely believed to be Michelangelo's crowning achievement in painting.

Claudia and Roger Kuttan at a colorful coir factory, at Alleppy, Kerala, in 1978. Coir is made from coconut husk.

Appu Kuttan holding Roger at the Plaque honoring the Kerala University athletic champions, including Appu Kuttan, at the University stadium in Trivandrum, Kerala, in 1978.

Roger Kuttan with his favorite coconut tree at Appu Kuttan's parents' home in Trivandrum, Kerala, in 1978.

Claudia and Roger Kuttan in front of the famous Taj Hotel in Bombay, in 1978.

Claudia and Roger Kuttan at the entrance to the stunningly beautiful and mystical Ajanta Buddhist Cave paintings and sculptures in 1978. Ajanta, a UNESCO World Heritage Centre, dating back to 200 B.C., is located in the state of Maharashtra.

Roger, Appu, and Claudia Kuttan at the scenic Mount Gulmarg, the Meadow of Flowers, in Kashmir, in 1978.

Appu, Roger, and Claudia Kuttan in front of the exquisitely carved, white marble Taj Mahal, the finest example of Mughal architecture, in 1978. Taj Mahal, located in Agra, is one of the Seven Wonders of the World.

Appu Kuttan and Roger enjoying a camel ride in Rajastan, in 1978.

Roger Kuttan at the Samurai Warrior Display in Tokyo, Japan, in 1978.

Roger and Appu Kuttan in Honolulu, Hawaii, a tropical paradise and a US state, at the conclusion of their world tour in 1978. The Polynesian Cultural Center is in the background.

Roger Kuttan with a park ranger in the majestic Grand Canyon National Park located in Arizona, in 1979. The Park is 446 km long and 29 km wide, and attains a depth of over 1.83 km. The walls of the Canyon, carved out by the Colorado River, reveal the geological story of Earth dating back to 500 million years.

Roger Kuttan at the famous Old Faithful Geyser in the 8,980 square km Yellowstone National Park in Wyoming, in 1979. The Park contains 60% of the world's geysers and is home to hundreds of wild animals including bears, buffaloes, elk, and moose. A wild buffalo can be seen grazing in the background.

Appu Kuttan holding Roger at Washburn Hot Springs located in Yellowstone National Park, in 1979. Washburn offers a unique perspective on Yellowstone, as it sits right at the edge of the Yellowstone Caldera. The views of wildflowers and the Canyon of Yellowstone are superb, and the chances of seeing wildlife, including bighorn sheep and bears, are excellent.

Roger with Claudia Kuttan at the Vishnu Schist, an overlook located in the Grand Canyon National Park, in 1979. The Vishnu Schist is a 1.7 billion year old Meta-sedimentary granite formation.

Roger Kuttan ready to go white water river rafting through the cliffs in the Western USA, in 1979.

Roger Kuttan with a park ranger at the fascinating Dinosaur National Monument in Utah, in 1979. The ranger is explaining how they extricate dinosaur fossils from the rocks. The monument contains one of the largest collections of dinosaur fossils anywhere.

Roger Kuttan with dinosaur models near the Dinosaur National Monument in Utah, in 1979.

Roger Kuttan at Sea World located in San Diego, California, in 1979. Sea World is a marine mammal theme park and oceanarium, with different rides, different shows with sharks, dolphins, and penguins as well as interactive programs with Beluga whales, dolphin encounters and several exhibits.

Claudia, Roger, and Appu Kuttan at the historic Spanish Missions National Park in San Antonio, Texas, in 1979. The Missions were established by the Catholic Church in the 18th Century along the San Antonio River.

Roger Kuttan in front of the Buddha statue at the Golden Gate Park in San Francisco, California, in 1979.

Roger Kuttan with Mickey Mouse at Disneyland in Anaheim, California, in 1979.

Appu Kuttan in New Delhi in 1980. Here, he is seen discussing his **Management By Systems (MBS)** strategy with top government officials.

Roger Kuttan started playing tennis since age 5. Here he is seen practising his tennis serve on the deck of his Washington, DC, home in 1981.

The eminent former Indian Supreme Court Justice Krishmaiyer (left) with his niece, Claudia and Roger Kuttan in Washington, DC, in the early 1980s.

Maya Kuttan at the celebration of her 1st birthday in 1982.

Maya Kuttan practicing the Tahitian dance she was taught at the Polynesian Cultural Center in Hawaii. In Hawaii, she wowed the large audience including, many Japanese tourists who stood in line afterwards to take photos with her.

World tennis champion Andre Agassi, practicing as a teenager, at the World-famous Nick Bollettieri Tennis Academy in Florida, USA. Appu Kuttan was the major shareholder and chairman of the Academy in the 1980s. He mentored Agassi since 1985.

World tennis champion Monica Seles in action at the Academy—notice her concentration on the ball. Appu Kuttan helped to bring the Seles family from Yugoslavia to the Academy in 1986. He has mentored her since then.

Roger Kuttan with his friend and world tennis champion Andre Agassi at the USA vs. Bahamas Davis Cup match in 1993.

World tennis champion Monica Seles with her friends, Maya and Roger Kuttan, at the Cyberlearning Center in Washington, DC, in 1995, when she announced her decision to return to tennis after a two year absence.

Roger and Appu Kuttan with world tennis champion Monica Seles and U.S. Congressman Tom Davis in Washington, DC, in 1995.

Roger Kuttan, with his sister Maya, after receiving MBA and JD (law) degrees from Stanford University, California, in 2002.

Appu Kuttan with daughter Maya at the debut of her award-winning film, *Shades of Crimson*, in Los Angeles, California, in 2005.

Appu Kuttan and Andre Agassi, World Tennis champion in Washington, DC, in 2008.

Maya Kuttan and Indian Nobel Laureate Rajendra Pachauri at the 2009 Global Climate Conference in Copenhagen, Denmark.

Maya Kuttan with family at her graduation from the University of California, Los Angeles (UCLA) Law School in 2010. From left to right: Appu Kuttan, Maya's fiancé Anthony Cann, Maya, Claudia and Roger Kuttan.

# CHAPTER 11

## PHILANTHROPIC
## FOUNDATION WORK

*"There is no better way to find happiness on this earth than helping those who need help, especially by providing them with educational opportunities!"*

## PRESIDENT BILL CLINTON HONOURS OUR SON, ROGER AND SUPPORTS OUR PLANS

IN 1993, President Bill Clinton honoured our son, Roger, during the United States Presidential Inauguration. As we attended several inaugural events, the President asked me how I was able to help our son and tennis champions such as Andre Agassi and Monica Seles reach world-class levels in such diverse arenas. I replied, "I look at everything as a system and everything can be improved through the systems approach, since existing systems become more ineffective and inefficient over time as per the principle of atrophy."

During those days, I also had conversations on digital education with Dr. Gordon Moore, co-founder of Intel. Soon after, I told my family that "I have good news and better news. The good news is that, with the support of President Clinton and Dr. Moore, I can help provide educational opportunities to thousands of disadvantaged students and adults. But the better news is that I am putting all the funds from the sale of the tennis academy to IMG, the multibillion-dollar sports management company, into the National Education Foundation (NEF) which I founded earlier to help bridge the academic and job skills divides."

My philosophy was to give our children the best education possible, and use my money to help provide educational and empowerment opportunities to the disadvantaged.

## I FOUNDED NEF AND COINED THE WORD "CYBERLEARNING"

I founded the non-profit National Education Foundation (NEF) in 1989. It became operational in 1993. The same year, I coined the word "cyberlearning" to describe learning via the Internet. I often say that "cyberlearning" is my contribution to the English language and dictionary. I am often referred to as the *father of cyberlearning*. Now, cyberlearning is used extensively by the United States' National Science Foundation as well as universities, non-governmental organizations, governments and corporations around the world.

In 1995, we kicked off a cyber-ed project from the White House, and took a 60-foot van equipped with high speed Internet-accessible computers to major cities across the United States, demonstrating to educators how cyberlearning can be used effectively for education. NEF's CyberLearning students also demonstrated to the United States Congress, in real time, how to solve free advanced math problems posted by universities on the Internet.

Since 1993, NEF has provided digital education opportunities to millions of disadvantaged students and adults in the United States, India, and many other countries. NEF has evolved into a global non-profit leader in bridging the digital, academic and employment divides.

NEF meets its mission by providing disadvantaged students and adults with significant educational opportunities through high-quality, affordable online education. Thus, NEF empowers them to gain 21st century skills, and thereby enables them, their families, communities and entire nations to thrive and live in a world free from poverty and terrorism.

## NEF PROJECTS
NEF fulfills its mission through three major projects:

1. **CyberLearning Academy** (*www.cyberlearning.org*) provides 21st century skills to disadvantaged students in Science, Technology, Engineering, Math (STEM), English, social studies, test preparation, information technology, business, and management in order to close the academic, digital and job skills divides;

The world-class Cyberlearning academy provides 6,000 high-quality, Web-based online courses offered through a state-of-the-art Learning Management System (LMS).

The LMS allows the academy directors and teachers to provide 24/7 unlimited course access to the students, track student activities and progress using pre- and post- tests in every course module, and generate real time reports for teachers, administrators, students and parents. These reports help to continuously monitor, evaluate and improve student performance.

In addition, the Cyberlearning academy provides a Total CyberLearning System Solution defined as **PSLMMTT**—Personalised learning, Stipends and bonuses for teachers based on performance, Learning Management System, Mentoring, Motivational rewards for students, teachers and parents, Teacher training and Tech support (24/7). The singular focus of the solution is helping each student improve his/her skills and scores.

To help nurture the body, mind and soul of the students, the Cyberlearning academy plans to offer thinking, physical education, and meditation programme options to participating schools.

In 2010, NEF implemented a grant programme to provide Online Math Homework Helper and digital literacy education to one million poor students across America. The academies, presently in 1,000-plus schools across the United States, have been very successful. NEF's goal is to set up CyberLearning Academies in most disadvantaged schools in the US and several in India by 2020.

For details visit www.cyberlearning.org.

2. **NEF University** provides tuition scholarships to jobseekers to access its online CyberLearning workforce training solutions and certifications in IT, soft skills, business, project management, office, test preparation, small business and other areas to close the skills gap. The immediate goal is to

train one million jobseekers in the United States. For details, visit *www. nefuniversity.org*.

3. **NEF International** provides tuition scholarships for digital literacy and workforce training to disadvantaged students and adults in many countries including India, Egypt and Mauritius. NEF offers 5,500 high-quality online courses in IT, and soft skills using a state-of-the-art Learning Management System (LMS).

I believe that training, certifying and placing unemployed college graduates in jobs in terror-prone countries provides the most cost-effective solution for reducing global terrorism. Such a solution could drastically reduce the number of potential leaders of terrorist groups.

## MIRACLE IN MAURITIUS IN MARCH

In February 2006, the Prime Minister of Mauritius, Dr. Navin Ramgoolam, invited me to meet him privately in Washington, DC. He said he learned from the Indian Ambassador in Mauritius about my work with Mr. Rajiv Gandhi to help make India an IT power. He added, "Mauritius is a small nation with a population of 1.3 million. Our economy is heavily dependent on tourism and sugarcane, both affected severely by the weather. How can you help us to become an ICT (Information and Communication Technology)-focused nation?"

I offered to go to Mauritius and assist him under the same two conditions I insisted on with Mr. Gandhi and other national leaders:

1. You don't pay me; if you pay, you are going to tell me what to do. If you don't pay me, and if you get the best team together, I can be a catalyst to help them set visions, missions, goals and objectives and come up with creative cost-effective solutions;

2. You must be serious about implementation.

The Prime Minister readily agreed to both conditions.

So, in March 2006, I went to Mauritius with my gracious and tech-savvy daughter, Maya. First, I met with the key leaders. Then I conducted a seminar for the entire Cabinet on Management By Systems (MBS). Third, I taught MBS to a working team consisting of government, public sector and private sector as well as academic leaders that the Prime Minister had put together.

Our first task was to define a vision for Mauritius. We agreed every country should take advantage of its niche strengths to compete in the 21$^{st}$ century global economy. We decided that Mauritius' niche strength is its location between India and Africa. So the team defined its vision as making Mauritius an Information and Communication Technology (ICT) bridge between ICT-advanced India and ICT-lagging Africa.

Once the vision was established, the team set the objective as creating a large pool of ICT professionals in Mauritius with globally recognised ICT certifications in Microsoft, Cisco, Oracle, etc., assuming that such a pool would attract investors and ICT companies from India, the United States, Europe and other countries.

To achieve the objective, the team set the system goal as training and certifying 400,000 Mauritians in the universally recognised digital literacy program—IC3 (Internet and Computer Core Certification)—in four years.

Thus, the output from the ICT educational system was defined as 400,000 IC3 graduates. To achieve that, the team decided to train all the high school and college students, all teachers, most public and private sector employees and some non-employees in IC3.

Using the **MBS** approach, the key resources required to transform the input (admitted students) to the output (IC3 graduates) were defined as FTTCMM (Facilities-Teacher/Trainer-Technology-Courseware/Certification-Mentoring-Motivation).

The team decided to upgrade the computer centre facilities at all the schools and train students during school hours and adults during non-school hours, including evenings and weekends. The University of Mauritius agreed to train teachers and trainers in IC3 at no cost to the government. The Government of India agreed to provide a low interest credit line to help the Mauritius Government purchase ICT products and services from India to upgrade hardware, software, system integration and Internet infrastructure in all school and government computer centres, thus helping to create a working technology system in Mauritius.

Our National Education Foundation (NEF) offered a multi-million dollar grant for IC3 and ICT courses as well as IC3 certification exams. The Prime Minister encouraged every ICT professional in Mauritius to mentor a few colleagues, friends and family members. Both the public and private sector companies offered to provide incentives such as salary increases for IC3 and ICT certified graduates.

The total programme cost came to much less than the market cost per trainee for courses and certifications in the three IC3 exams. This is only a fraction of the normal cost elsewhere in the world. The team decided to charge that cost as a fee to every trainee except the students; the government made passing the IC3 course mandatory for college admission and agreed to pay the IC3 fee for high school students.

## THE PRIME MINISTER PRESENTS MAURITIUS' PLAN

Once the team completed its work in three weeks, the Prime Minister presented it to the country in a nationally televised speech. I was then asked to go on national TV to explain the project. Thus, in March 2006, Mauritius changed its economic focus—a remarkable national achievement by any standard! This shows that bold visionary leaders can make a significant difference in the lives of their people. The Prime Minister of Mauritius deserves congratulations for pulling off a miracle in just three weeks! See www.cyberlearningmauritius.org.

The Prime Minister's Universal ICT programme was officially launched in September, 2006. The National Computer Board, a government entity in Mauritius, has trained tens of thousands of students and adults since then. In early 2010, the Cabinet declared total satisfaction with the first phase of the project implementation and authorised the start of the second phase, namely ICT professional certifications, with a grant from our National Education Foundation (NEF).

It is expected that the second phase of the project will help create an adequate pool of qualified ICT professionals who will contribute to the economic growth of the country. Phase two will cover training in IT and business certifications including Microsoft, Cisco, Oracle, Web Design, IT security and Project Management.

## MILLION INDIANS INFORMATION TECHNOLOGY EDUCATION (MIITE) PROJECT

In 1980, while advising Mr. Rajiv Gandhi to devise a strategy to make India an IT power, I told him that one day I hope to help train a million underprivileged Indians, especially women and minorities, in IT and soft skills.

Recently I went to India to discuss the Million Indians Information Technology Education (MIITE) project with Indian leaders. I felt that the timing was right, since India needs millions of IT workers to stay on top in the global IT arena. The MIITE programme will help bridge the enormous digital and employment divides in India by providing opportunities for high-quality, affordable IT and soft skills education, leading to jobs for many underprivileged Indians, especially women and minorities, who are seriously underrepresented in India's IT and executive workforce.

The goal of the MIITE project is to train a million disadvantaged Indians in IT and soft skills, starting in 2013. Our non-profit National Education Foundation (NEF) has offered to provide support for the project.

NEF has devised a unique strategy to fund part of the cost. We have invited Indian corporations, US corporations with Indian subsidiaries and other entities interested in our India mission to use our top-quality online and blended (online plus onsite) training services at a cost 50% to 80% below market cost, as global leaders such as Lockheed Martin and Wipro have done. We can then use those funds for implementing the MIITE programme. We can also sponsor colleges or towns in India selected by the corporate participants in their corporate names and at no cost to the colleges.

The benefits to the participants include significant savings in their training costs as well as good local, regional and national PR/publicity in India, and CSR (Corporate Social Responsibility) credit.

As an added bonus, employers who use the NEF training services for 5,000 or more employees can sponsor colleges or universities in India. I may then personally visit those institutions and give motivational talks and demonstrations to students on the Happy Executive concept of developing a mind, body, and soul nurturing lifestyle. As a 72-year-old former university athletics champion, I hope to inspire young and old alike to stay in shape and in balance physically, mentally and spiritually.

We are also planning to offer affordable MIITE programmes through colleges and universities. Interested academic, corporate and other institutions are welcome to contact us. For details, visit *www.cyberlearning.org/india* or my personal websites *www.appuji.org* or *www.happyexecutive.org*.

The MIITE project has two missions:

1.  To level the playing field by giving every Indian an equal opportunity to get IT/soft skills education/training.

2.  To help keep India at the top of the global IT arena. I used to tell world tennis champions, Andre Agassi and Monica Seles, both of whom I mentored, that it is harder to stay on top than to get to the top!

We hope to launch the MIITE project nationally in India in 2013.

I believe the Happy Executive practices will help India's executives and youngsters to stay in excellent condition to create jobs and successfully compete for jobs in the global economy, while maintaining their spiritual values.

In the following chapter, I look at India as a system, and propose pathway guidance for Indian leaders, executives and non-executives alike, to build a strong and happy India.

Appu Kuttan with Prime Minister Indira Gandhi at the Indian Embassy in Washington, DC, in 1982.

Prime Minister Rajiv Gandhi and his wife Sonia Gandhi and their children Priyanka and Rahul in the US, in 1985. (Courtesy of Rajan Devadas)

Appu Kuttan and son Roger Kuttan with President Bill Clinton at the US Presidential Inauguration in 1993. Roger was selected by the President as a **'Face of Hope'** to represent the young Americans at the Inauguration.

National Education Foundation Vice President Roger Kuttan (left) discussing the missions of the Foundation with First Daughter Chelsea Clinton at a White House function in 1993.

Roger Kuttan discussing matters of interest to young Americans with President Bill Clinton, in 1993. He was featured in a front cover story in February, 1993 by *The Week*, a national magazine in India. The story under the title **"Indian prodigy charms Clinton,"** featured pictures of Roger with President Clinton, President Clinton's daughter Chelsea Clinton, World tennis champion Monica Seles and World famous singer Michael Jackson.

Appu Kuttan (in the middle) and Roger (far right) with the Cyberlearning middle school team after their presentation on "Math Learning via the Internet," to the US Congress in 1996.

Appu Kuttan congratulates Collier County School District's Cyberlearning Academy director Grace Vaknin for significantly improving the student math and IT scores and skills using the top quality Cyberlearning online courses as well as effective mentoring and motivational programs provided by Cyberlearning. Collier County is located in Florida.

Appu Kuttan being congratulated by the Mauritius Prime Minister Navin Ramgoolam in 2006 for helping to design and implement the Prime Minister's Universal ICT Project to transform Mauritius from a sugarcane and tourism based economy to an ICT-focused nation. The National Education Foundation has provided tuition scholarships to train 400,000 Mauritians in digital literacy and ICT. The project has become a model for developing countries.

One of the several Cyberlearning Academies across the United States in operation. The National Education Foundation's mission is to set up top quality K-12 Cyberlearning academies in most disadvantaged schools in the United States by 2020. The Foundation provides a Total Cyberlearning System Solution including individualized learning courses, mentoring, motivational rewards, teacher training and tech support to improve student skills and scores in math, English, science, social studies, IT (including 60 certifications), business and test prep.

Appu Kuttan with daughter Maya in Mauritius in 2006, as guests of Mauritius Prime Minister Naveen Ramglooam.

Appu Kuttan receiving the **Global Digital Literacy Champion Award** from Certiport CEO David Saedi in 2006. The award was given to the person who contributed most to improve digital literacy in the world.

Appu Kuttan started discussing his dream project to train a million Indians in IT since 2006. Here he is seen discussing the project with Indian President Abdul Kalam.

# PART III:

# A SYSTEMS APPROACH FOR INDIA

# CHAPTER 12

## A PATHWAY FOR INDIAN LEADERS, EXECUTIVES AND NON-EXECUTIVES – A CALL TO ACTION!

*"Each one of us must first learn to live a healthy and happy life, taking the best from the West in technology and science, and balancing it with our traditional spiritual values rooted in caring, love, compassion and sharing."*

## THE ROLE OF INDIAN YOUTH

India is extremely significant in the global economic system. Why do I say that? Young people in India represent the future not just of India, but of the entire world! The 21st century can truly be an Indian Century, if Indian leaders and people live up to their potential.

It is predicted that by 2040, one out of every three workers in the world could be Indian. The sheer size of what has been referred to as the *youth bulge*—an estimated 240 million youths in India coming to working age in the next 20 years is mind boggling. Currently, nearly two-thirds of India's population is younger than 35—the largest pool of young people in the world. In contrast, China's population of 1.3 billion, through its one-child-per-family policy, is slowly turning grey. The average age of workers in the West and in Japan is already much higher than that in India.

It is truly astounding to think that half of India's population is now under 24, and will form the backbone of the world's largest and potentially one of the most vibrant democracies. What this enormous demographic group does in the next 20 years will shape the future of India and the world in the 21st century. The actions of the Indian youth—how they manage time, save and spend money, eat, exercise, think and make decisions as well as their spiritual, ethical and political values—are critical to the success of both the Indian and global welfare.

You may be one of those who can shape the future as an employer, employee, or parent of a young person on the rise. This book is meant to help you to understand the facts, your calling and your pathway to success.

# INDIA'S ROLE IN THE 21ST CENTURY

India is truly at a crossroad in its history. While I was growing up in post-Independence India, there was considerable doubt about the future of the country. Could India feed and sustain itself, and could its new democratic system manage to reconcile the competing demands of the country's diverse groups and ethnic minorities? Was India going to follow an independent foreign policy, and could it ever escape from the tensions with Pakistan and in Kashmir?

All these were open questions then. Some have been notably addressed, yet most are still a work-in-progress. It would have been hard to imagine at that time, that 65 years later, India could be positioned to become a world superpower. This achievement has been phenomenal. Since 1985, the country has lifted 431 million people out of poverty, and many millions have entered the middle class.

According to the latest Forbes survey, 48 Indians have joined the ranks of the world's richest billionaires. Recently, one of these billionaires asked me to advise him on creating a legacy programme for him.

The challenge for India is to continue sensibly the trends it began in the 1980s, when Prime Minister Rajiv Gandhi opened India to information technology and Western cooperation. I had the good fortune of advising Mr. Gandhi on laying a vision to make India an IT power before he became Prime Minister.

India can be a global superpower in the 21st century, if young Indians adopt and use the latest advances in science and technology effectively, while maintaining India's traditional spiritual values. The two factors that can alter the equation are global warming and terrorism. Reducing India's carbon footprint and finding peace with Pakistan and in Kashmir are critical tasks facing young Indians.

In 1980, I advised a young Rajiv Gandhi that the next few decades would be dominated by IT (Information Technology). Now, I tell world leaders that the next few decades will be dominated by the four T's, namely, IT, ET (Energy Technology), BT (Bio Technology), and FT (Food Technology including Water). Hence, India should embark on an ambitious, concerted programme of developing and applying IT, ET, BT and FT for mass use, as China has already started doing.

India should establish 21$^{st}$ century centres via government programmes as well as corporate, NGO and public-private partnerships to foster innovation and deployment of IT, ET, BT and FT. This can be done all over India, especially around the IITs, IIMs and other top universities, by following the example of Silicon Valley in the United States, which developed around Stanford and other universities.

In addition, the following is a list of five critical areas and objectives I think are necessary for India to advance in the 21$^{st}$ Century. I call them the Five Pillars for A Happy India.

## <u>Pillar 1</u>

### — Education

It is well understood that education is the key to empowerment everywhere. Historically, people with better education have had more opportunities for employment and advancement, and have consequently led a more fulfilling and enriched life. This, in turn, gave them more happiness and the ability to lead a healthier life for themselves and their loved ones.

The higher your education level, the more money you make. According to the United States Census Bureau, an average college graduate in the United States earns twice as much money as a high school graduate. A recent Swedish study concludes that people who are educated for at least nine years have a lower mortality rate than those who study for eight years or less.

In spite of the recent economic progress, India faces a monumental challenge in education, in terms of both quantity and quality.

According to a recent UNESCO report, India has 21 million children who are not enrolled in primary schools, and about 50% of the eligible youth are not enrolled in high schools. To meet its ever expanding workforce demand, India needs thousands of new schools and colleges. According to India's Ministry of Human Resource Development, India needs 1,000 new universities and 50,000 new colleges to prepare 100 million additional Indian youth entering the workforce by 2020. It is estimated that India needs millions of skilled professionals in all areas including IT, healthcare, manufacturing, management, business, entrepreneurship, and vocational trades.

In fact, fewer than 60% of grade five students in India can read, and can do basic math at grade two level. About 40% of children starting school are malnourished, and this affects their ability to learn. Only 40% of students go on to high school, with 15% graduating from high school, and 7% graduating from college. Compare that with the college graduation rates of 56% for Canada and South Korea.

Only 25% of Indian college graduates readily find jobs. Graduates of the IITs and IIMs are considered to be among the best in the world, and get many job offers, but graduates of lower tier universities and colleges need additional training to get employment. These institutions should do more to prepare their students to meet the job skills requirements of prospective employers.

India should develop local, statewide, regional and national databases to match jobs and required job skills, with the appropriate education and training provided by educational institutions. All educational institutions should be required to post all relevant information transparently about courses, teachers, graduation rates, job placement rates and fees on their websites, so that potential students and their families can make better decisions.

India needs to invest in Education at all levels. I call this K-99 learning (meaning kindergarten to senior citizens), since the 21ˢᵗ century requires life-long learning. In this endeavour, India must promote active participation of all organizations and individuals including government, the public and private sectors, nonprofits, academic institutions and others.

The quality of course materials in India is poor in public schools and colleges. Governments must make quality books and online course materials affordable for all students. States should make the highest quality courses available to all schools via the Internet. All Indian colleges should be given access to top quality online courses from top universities such as Harvard, MIT, Stanford, IITs and IIMs. Many such courses are freely available on the internet. This will level the playing field, and ensure that all college and university students have access to the best course materials.

Teacher training must be upgraded and vastly expanded. About half of India's teachers are not trained. To remedy this situation, the government should do the following:

- Establish teacher training programmes in colleges and universities;

- Certify teachers through statewide exams;

- Phase in state certification as a requirement to be employed as a teacher;

- Provide grants and low interest loans to students who enroll in teacher training programmes;

- Use a blended learning approach, meaning using online courses and on-site teachers, to train teachers for 1,000 new universities and 50,000 new colleges;

- Utilize online teacher training course materials from top global universities such as Columbia University's Teachers College;

- Train and certify a number of master teachers, who will then train and certify a number of second level master teachers and so on. Implement this "train the trainer" approach nationally, regionally, statewide and locally.

Teachers must be motivated to teach at a high quality level. Salaries for teachers must be increased. Other incentives such as performance-based bonuses will help to motivate teachers. Actions must be taken to reduce the high 25% plus absenteeism rate of teachers in Indian public schools.

To avoid social unrest due to unequal educational opportunities, India must bring high quality education to all urban and rural area schools. This can be done. For example, high quality course materials can be made available via the internet to all students and teachers of schools and colleges, as many public, private and nonprofit organizations including our foundation are doing in the United States. Universal high quality online courses can be provided to all students only by improving the infrastructure, including physical facilities, water and electricity, as well as providing internet-accessible computers in all schools and colleges.

Remember, in any "K-99" learning system, the goal is to transform admitted students meeting specific eligibility requirements to graduating students meeting specific skill requirements. All resources including human, financial, information, technology, physical, material and time must be cost-effectively deployed.

To achieve India's education potential, all parties—union government, state governments, local governments, politicians, public and private sectors, NGOs, and academic institutions—must work together diligently. Serious efforts must be made to drastically reduce the prevailing significant negative influence of politicians and communal leaders on education in India. Without a good education system and skilled workforce, India will not be able to compete effectively in the 21st century global economy.

On a personal note, I am in the process of developing a mind-body-soul nurturing "Appuji" holistic education system for three to six year-old children. Such a system can instill the love of thinking and learning in children. It will also introduce them to a healthy and happy lifestyle from an early age. I hope this system will help change and improve early childhood education in India for the better. Imagine if every child develops a healthy and happy lifestyle from the very beginning! India and the world would be far better off in terms of both peace and prosperity.

There are many things that you, as a 21$^{st}$ century employee or employer, can do right now to prepare yourself for advancement during your entire working career. These are some suggestions you might find helpful:

- Many jobs in the years ahead are not even known now. Whenever you have an opportunity to learn on the job, take advantage of it;

- Whatever you can learn on your own from reading or taking courses on the internet etc., do it. Besides courses in your field, always consider taking courses in basic IT and business skills and applications;

- Also, take soft skills courses, including both verbal and written communications, marketing, business and entrepreneurship. Improving your soft skills will also give you the tools to create your own business from your ideas. Being able to communicate effectively is important to market yourself and your ideas or products or services.

## Pillar 2

## — Healthcare

People of the Indian sub-continent have a genetic predisposition to diabetes, high blood pressure and high cholesterol, all of which lead to early incapacity, strokes, heart attacks, organ failure and blindness. Indians cannot risk following the West blindly in all matters, especially in consuming the convenience-based fast foods and sugary drinks, and adopting the sedimentary lifestyle that involves little walking and other physical activity. Indians must also cut down on smoking and excessive alcohol consumption, since smoking leads to cancer, excessive alcohol leads to loss of liver and brain cells, and both lead to a shorter lifespan.

This stressful, hurried pathway to instant gratification leads to an overall poorer quality of life, including health problems such as diabetes and heart diseases at younger ages, with more disruptions and less happiness and peace at home, in the workplace, and in society.

People, especially the young, need to think through the consequences of following some of the negative trends of western lifestyles and attitudes. We only have to look at the increasing obesity and diabetes statistics to signal some alarm bells. Today an estimated 51 million Indians have diabetes, and 150 million have pre-diabetes, placing an alarmingly growing healthcare cost burden on India. The acceleration in diabetes, high blood pressure, and high cholesterol is primarily the result of more disposable income being used to buy the mostly unhealthy food (high fat, sugar, salt) and drinks that are now being so readily consumed all across India.

Motorcycles and relatively inexpensive cars are readily available, allowing many Indians to drive everywhere, just as most Americans do. Malls seem to be growing at a fast pace, providing easy access to packaged, processed foods and fast foods. Even Indians with a modest income have mobile phones which are used to order unhealthy fast food.

This combination of eating unhealthy food and reducing physical activity leads to poorer health, less productivity and less happiness. Young people should take steps to face this serious problem and make changes now before it is too late. Ruined health cannot be restored easily. Remember the wise saying —*an ounce of prevention is better than a pound of cure.*

At a time when millions of middle-class Indians are splurging on fast food, processed food, sweets and sugar-laden drinks as well as motorcycles and cars, 45% of Indian children under five suffer from malnutrition, according to the World Bank. Can India achieve its vision with 45% of its children suffering from stunted growth and brain damage caused by malnutrition?

We have lost sight of some of our guiding values. The medical establishment, governments and well-intentioned media have no real way of dealing with the sophisticated marketing of fast food, packaged food and soft drink companies. After all, who can argue with the price and the convenience? It is all too easy to get caught up with these perceived signs of progress and status. Being part of this westernised materialistic "me generation," "instant gratification" lifestyle also prevents us from looking out for others—thinking about the spiritual, caring, compassionate aspects of our lives. In such a scenario, every moment is filled with noise, busyness and other distractions.

Young Indians can be easily swept up into what is perceived as the "false" magic bus to more prosperity and happiness. We need not sacrifice the traditions and spirituality of our culture to achieve our economic goals.

I realise I am one voice against a tidal wave, a veritable tsunami of commercial messages created to persuade us to part with our money, while trying to convince us that the object of life is to assemble as many materialistic things and shallow experiences as we can before we die. Our lives will become pretty dull and empty if we decide to take that route.

## Pillar 3

### — Environment

Climate Change is a serious problem facing the planet. Very recently, a United Nations panel of climate experts projected that sea levels globally will rise twice as fast as previously predicted due to the accelerated melting of glaciers in Antarctica and Greenland, resulting from global warming. The likely result would be the loss of coastal areas across the globe including India.

India is very vulnerable. We must act to reduce global warming, and especially India's carbon footprint. During the next few years, the glaciers in the Himalayas will melt at a faster rate and send waters crashing down the Ganges and several other rivers, causing severe floods. During the decades following the floods, there would be unprecedented drought conditions that could lead to the starvation of hundreds of millions and the possible ruination of our economy, democratic government and culture.

Indian youth can be world leaders in developing new forms of green energy sources, so that the 45% of Indians who remain off the grid can also enjoy the benefits of modern life, health and education. We must help to reduce the world's dependence on oil, and eliminate India's import of 70% of the nation's carbon-based energy needs. We can revolutionise Indian agriculture, which is not very productive, because of the failure to innovate and manage food and water effectively—problems that will only get worse in the coming years due to climate change.

Each one of us can and must start adopting consumption patterns leading to a sustainable energy lifestyle.

## Pillar 4

### — Transportation, Communication, and Infrastructure

Inadequate infrastructure presents a challenge for any country because it inhibits development, and results in underutilized or wasted resources. Businesses cannot thrive because they cannot bring their goods to market, and individuals cannot access the tools and means to improve their lives.

In order to maintain the rapid pace of economic growth in India, physical, electric and electronic connectivity is vitally important.

The transportation sector accounted for 5.5% of GDP in 2007, the largest share of which came from road transportation. India is also known for its railways, which carry 17 million passengers and 2 million tons of freight per day. In recent years, air travel has expanded considerably. There are now 125 airports, 20 of which are international, transporting 96 million passengers and 1.5 tons of cargo per year.

India has also seen large investments in electricity and telecommunications in recent decades. It now has the second-largest mobile phone user base, with 930 million users, and has the world's third largest internet user base, with 121 million. This industry contributes nearly 350,000 crore (US $70 billion) to GDP.

Despite these strengths, India faces serious challenges when it comes to transportation, communication, and infrastructure. India's roads are congested and in disrepair. Only 1/3 of road maintenance needs are funded. Rural areas still have poor road access, leaving millions without all-weather roads. Capacity is lacking on the railways and in the ports.

The IT sector has played a central role in the nation's economic output, Yet only 10.2% of households possess internet access and only 1.18% have broadband access. The decentralized nature of the telecom and power sectors raises concerns about security, stability, and the nation's ability to recover from disasters or problems.

India needs to increase current levels of investment in infrastructure. The modernizing, expanding, and integration of the nation's transportation and communication systems, will create new capacity and growth for subsequent decades and generations, and will provide much needed jobs for the Indian youth. India should focus on providing a stable and secure infrastructure that will attract businesses which may be unwilling to invest otherwise. Pragmatic regulations are needed to achieve this stability, while encouraging private investment.

To compete in the global economy, India must significantly improve its transportation and communication capabilities. Witness the fact that China launched the world's fastest train capable of traveling at 300 kph, in December of 2012!

India should view its communication and transportation infrastructure as vital investments with implications not only on economic growth, but also on distance education, health services, and social justice.

## Pillar 5

### — Governance and Social Justice

The concept of social justice is central to India's continued development. It is not only found in the opening words of the Indian constitution, but it has implications for economic growth as well. To maximize productivity, a nation must give adequate opportunities to all of its citizens and fully utilize its human resources. This cannot occur without social justice. The means by which this goal can be achieved is good governance.

Every effort must be made to eradicate corruption, and make governance transparent, effective, and efficient. It should bring the majority of the population, including the villagers and the underprivileged, into the mainstream by giving them better education, nutrition, healthcare, job opportunities and hope. If India can grow its economy at 7% to 8% per year now, with less than 20% of the population actively involved, imagine what India can achieve when the vast majority of Indians are brought into the mainstream!

The current state of corruption in India does not induce faith or trust in government institutions. A 2005 study found that 62% of Indians had experienced influence peddling or bribes to get projects completed in public offices. In 2008 the number was down to 40%, indicating some progress in this regard. However, India still ranks 95th out of 178 countries in Transparency International's Corruption Perceptions Index, and 120 of India's 523 parliament members were facing criminal charges as of 2008.

Many scandals, like the 2010 Commonwealth Games scam, the 2G spectrum scam, the Adarsh Housing Society scam, and the recent Coal Mining scam have gone all the way to the top levels of government, including Cabinet Ministers and Chief Ministers. Although India's economic growth has lifted extraordinary numbers of people out of poverty, the conditions have declined for certain minority groups. The Dalit caste and Adivasi tribe have been especially isolated and negatively impacted. The needs of these groups have not been adequately addressed by the government, and without trust in government institutions, the people have little reason to believe the problems will be solved in the future. In order to provide justice, empowerment, employment, and efficiency to all Indians, India must continue to improve its governance. Prime Minister Manmohan Singh has been outspoken against corruption. Yet his government seems to be engulfed in several allegations of corruption. Efforts are underway in  Parliament to improve judicial accountability and protect whistle blowers, but sweeping major steps are needed urgently and rapidly.

The steps India has taken already to root out corruption and improve social justice are admirable, but must be vastly expanded. India should increase the political participation of minority groups and women, and continue to decentralize and democratize government power by delegating more authority to local governments. Elections should be publicly funded, and there must be transparency and competition in procurement and government contracts. Government must invest in infrastructure and expand access to education, especially in areas with higher concentrations of underprivileged minority groups. These steps will help provide opportunities for disadvantaged populations, restore trust in government, and achieve social justice for all Indians, as the constitution intended.

India must guarantee the rights of every citizen, including minorities and women. The recent widespread national rape protests indicate that India urgently needs reform and strict enforcement of laws governing equality, rights and justice at the local, state and national levels.

## INDIA'S ULTIMATE GOAL

The ultimate vision for India must be to use its growing economic power to bring all Indians to a higher level of fulfillment and happiness. This means providing everyone adequate nutrition, education, healthcare, employment, culture, recreation, self-confidence, and most of all, hope. The focus of governments at all levels should be not only improving Gross Domestic Product (GDP), but also the Gross Happiness Product (GHP).

To achieve the above objective, every Indian must first learn to live a healthy and happy life, taking the best from the West in technology and science, and balancing it with Indian traditional spiritual values rooted in caring, love, compassion and sharing.

To achieve its potential, India must address the problems of the two-thirds of Indians who live in the villages. Their lives have not been affected much by India's economic upsurge. It is time to create public-private sector partnerships to develop and implement creative, holistic sustainable solutions to improve the quality of life of the villagers—by giving them opportunities to nurture their mind, body and soul. I have been urging Indian leaders to set up a Mind-Body-Soul model pilot centre in a village or cluster of villages in India, and then replicate it throughout India.

The 21st century could be the Indian Century, if people like you, who read this book, apply the lessons contained in this book. It can seem overwhelming if you take up this challenge all at once.

What I advocate is that social change begins with you and me, exercising personal discipline in our daily choices and routines. It is imperative that we develop first our individual potential, and then our collective potential as members of society, if we want to keep the gains we have made, and capitalise on them for a healthy, prosperous and happy India. Our goal should and could be to live a life full of potential, health and happiness.

## Message to the reader:

**Thank you for reading this *Happy Executive* book. Please visit my websites, www.appuji.org and www.happyexecutive.org for more motivational messages, practical suggestions and updates. Enjoy a happier and healthier life every day!**

**— Dr. Appu Kuttan**

www.appuji.org
www.happyexecutive.org
www.cyberlearning.org
www.nefuniversity.org

Made in the USA
Charleston, SC
16 June 2015